DOGS NEED
OUR LOVE

DOGS NEED OUR LOVE

by

Jack L. Tuttle, DVM, M.Ed.

LIBRA PUBLISHERS, INC.

The drawings in this book were prepared by Mr. Jerry Barrett.

First Edition

Library of Congress Catalog No. 82-082547

Copyright © 1983 by Jack L. Tuttle, DVM, M. Ed.

All rights reserved

Libra Publishers, Inc.
391 Willets Road
Roslyn Heights, New York 11577

Manufactured in the United States of America

ISBN 0-87212-163-1

To Ginger, Tory, Tuffy and Christopher, my best teachers

Table of Contents

INTRODUCTION

This is a book about dogs, but it is also about people. The typical pet dog has been selected, bred, and domesticated to be dependent on people. Our interest in dog behavior is the result of problems which arise when dogs and people interact. Thus, we can best learn about pet dogs by studying their relationships with people and the major role we play in influencing their behavior.

The study of dog behavior is in its infancy, and we have much to learn. Several excellent books have been written on dog behavior, based on scientific research. However, most of these books examine the dog as a separate entity and ignore the influence of people on dog behavior.

Many of these books are also of limited practical value to the average pet owner. They use technical jargon that is often too complex for most people. They tend to separate behaviors into a variety of neat categories, each with a regimented set of procedures designed for behavior modification. But if we were to follow all these guidelines as suggested, we would have time for little else, and our desire for dogs as pets and family members would quickly fade.

Many dog behavior books emphasize training techniques too heavily. Certainly, most dogs can be trained to perform a few tricks and obey commands from people who are natural leaders. But many of us are unable or unwilling to function as leaders. Training techniques then have little value.

Dogs have served humans well for many centuries. They provide great assistance and solace to children, the elderly, and the physically and mentally handicapped. There are guide dogs, hunting dogs, herding dogs, police dogs, sled dogs, racing dogs, attack dogs, guard dogs and show dogs. And many dogs serve as their owners' most trusted companions.

The question is, have we done enough to return the favor? We provide food, shelter, and veterinary services, but then we blame dogs if they do not conform to our standards. We want them to help us, but we expect them to behave like people instead of dogs. How can we help them unless we recognize their right to be dogs, not humans?

Dogs are not just machines that we can turn on and off at will. Some dogs will always refuse to submit, even to the most dominant people. And some dogs are harmed when forced to serve a submissive role at all times. Yet there is a way that both dogs and people can benefit from each other.

The key to a beneficial relationship between dogs and people is *understanding*. We must understand what dogs are really like, and we must also understand how dogs perceive us. Above all else, dogs need love; and the kind of love they need can be provided only with understanding.

This book is designed to help people understand their dogs better, and thereby to love them more

DOGS NEED
OUR LOVE

Chapter 1

NORMAL OR ABNORMAL?

When a child throws a temper tantrum, we usually consider it normal and temporary. But when a dog chews up the furniture, many people fear brain impairment or a deep psychological disturbance. A temper tantrum is usually a frustration reaction, and so is destructive chewing. Only our perception of the two events differs.

Certainly, some dogs suffer brain disorders which alter their behavior. But brain defects and psychological disturbances are less common in dogs than people. Some dogs can be classified as neurotic or psychotic, and some suffer from diseases and hereditary abnormalities such as epilepsy and hydrocephalus (water on the brain). This is especially true of some popular dog breeds which have been inbred excessively for their profit potential. However, the vast majority of dogs have no major physical or mental problems which alter their behavior.

Most of the time, dog behavior "problems" are normal, predictable responses to changes in the environment. As pet owners, we may dislike these behaviors. We want our dogs to be part of our lives, but we grow intolerant when they behave like dogs instead of people. Many normal, healthy dogs are brought to veterinarians for neurological examinations as a result of their behavior changes. Many more are given away, thrown out of their homes, or euthanized because their behavior bothers their owners. The real problem is often our inability to accept and understand normal dog behavior. Only our expectations are abnormal. For example, some people like to brag that their dogs do not bite. Others claim their dogs would never engage in sex. In reality, all dogs bite if they sense they are in jeopardy. And sexual drives during mating season almost always supersede human sensibilities on the subject. Owners who deny these realities have unrealistic expectations that dogs cannot fulfill.

It seems that many dog owners are quick to blame their dogs for behaviors which are normal.

Like people, no dog can behave exactly the same at all times. And a dog may react well to one person, but poorly to another. Dogs have both good days and bad days.

From a dog's perspective, a person is a part of the environment. How it reacts to that person depends on whether it perceives the person as friend or foe. Many negative behaviors result when a dog detects an enemy. Incompatibility with its owner is a principal cause of dog behavior problems. We may blame our dogs for behaving poorly, but our own inconsistencies may have caused the behavior change in the first place. After all, no argument is one-sided.

Even highly unusual behaviors may be normal in certain dogs, as one of my cases indicates. A two-year-old male Doberman had periodic episodes of snapping its teeth violently at imaginary objects. The owners thought their dog was hallucinating and having epileptic seizures. But while some signs of epilepsy were present, a neurological examination proved normal. In addition, routine treatment with anticonvulsive drugs brought no improvement. The owners then remembered that their dog always calmed down when the husband held and loved it. In fact, both owners would rush to comfort the dog whenever its episodes began.

To test whether the dog was just trying to get attention, the owners ignored the fits, but gave the dog plenty of attention when it behaved normally. The episodes ceased completely within a week. Evidently, one brief hallucination had proved a valuable attention-getter when the owners overreacted. The dog quickly learned to behave as if hallucinating to get attention. With time and repetition, its behavior actually came to seem like epilepsy, even though the dog was normal.

All dogs have survival needs, which they must fulfill daily through instinctive reflex reactions to changes in their environment. These instincts are too strong to change. We create survival conflicts for dogs by attempting to change them. To enjoy good relationships with our dogs, we must understand their survival needs and their normal tendencies. And just as important, we must understand how dogs perceive us.

Most behaviorists agree that dogs have no conscious control

over their actions. They have coined a number of technical names for the different reflex responses that dogs demonstrate. In doing so, they have striven to distinguish between a dog's instincts and a person's conscious decisions. Most behaviorists refuse to use terms like jealousy, revenge, and resentment to describe a dog's behavior.

However, such terms will be used in this book. For one thing, most of us understand human emotions without memorizing the jawbreaking jargon psychologists use to describe them. Simplicity enhances our understanding.

Secondly, it is more important to understand the functional realities of behavior than to adhere to the niceties of terminology. For example, if a parent favors one child over another, the second child may become jealous and try to regain the parent's attention. Likewise, when a dog owner favors one dog over another, the second dog may act as if jealous and try to regain the owner's attention. The second child and the second dog may behave in similar ways to elevate their positions in their families, with similar results. It doesn't really matter whether these behaviors are reflexes or consciously controlled, since both the cause and result are practically identical.

If your dog's behavior is truly abnormal, see your veterinarian. But if your dog is merely throwing a temper tantrum, treat it as such. A method for controlling temper tantrums in children will probably work well with your dog, too.

Chapter 2

INSTINCTS AND SURVIVAL NEEDS

Instincts are reflex patterns of behavior which are inherited and cannot be changed or eliminated. They are powerful drives which dogs must follow to fulfill basic survival needs such as procuring food, protecting themselves, and reproducing to ensure the species survival. All dogs are born with two basic instincts which enable them to survive in the face of danger: they either fight it or flee from it. The fight reflex stems from the dog's feeling of superiority or control. Fighting is one of many behaviors which demonstrate a dominant character. The flight reflex produces an escape from danger and occurs out of fear. Thus, it is a submissive trait.

Every dog is born with both dominant and submissive drives, but the ability to balance both varies from one dog to another. Every dog will demonstrate one of these two drives for each change in its environment, but how often it shows dominance or submission will be slightly different from any other dog.

Dominant and submissive instincts are truly opposites, even though survival can be furthered each time either drive is acted upon. Since these instinctive needs are constant, dogs consistently able to satisfy both are content and behave predictably. But behavior problems can result when a dog is in conflict over a need to satisfy both instincts at the same time.

Dominant dogs are independent leader types, while submissive dogs are dependent followers. The most dominant dogs have few submissive drives, and the most submissive dogs have few dominant drives, but both instincts are always present. In fact, every dog needs to be both a leader and a follower. Dogs require opportunities to be independent, but they also crave the security provided by a more respected leader. Any dog forced to be only a leader or only a follower will become emotionally unstable.

The ability to live requires a will to live. The will to live increases with a dog's confidence in its ability to survive, and it decreases when a dog loses confidence by its inability to use its survival instincts to best advantage. Although winning a fight or escaping from danger increases survival potential, the most confident dogs are the dominant, independent types who fight successfully and fear little. They serve as leaders and provide security for more submissive, fearful dogs. Fearful dogs need to run away less when more confident leaders are there to protect them.

This dominant-submissive relationship is the basis for dog pack behavior. Like wolves and coyotes, dogs have survived over the centuries by living in groups. The most dominant dog is the pack leader, who assists the less dominant members of the group. On the whole, dogs are somewhat submissive because of their dependence on group activity for food and security. This dependence contrasts with the highly independent, asocial nature of, for example, wild cats.

The need for a leader is the primary reason dogs first befriended people many centuries ago, and this instinctive drive continues today. Dogs look to people as their pack leaders, and we respond by providing them with food, shelter, security, and love. This is generally a mutually beneficial relationship. A dog's need to follow and a person's need to lead can both be satisfied.

However, conflicts arise for dogs when we provide inconsistent leadership. One big reason for these conflicts is that many people have dependency needs of their own. As a result, they may need their dog more than the dog needs them. Such people are perceived as poor leaders by the average pet dog.

Another major reason for conflict results from a lack of understanding of the dog's true nature. We can help dogs acquire or eliminate certain behaviors, but only if changes are compatible with their natural tendencies and beneficial to their survival. We cannot change dogs' natures, although many of us try hard to do so.

We cannot turn a fearful dog into a confident watch dog. We cannot force a highly dominant dog to submit to us at all times. We cannot force dogs to ignore mating season. To try to change a dog's normal tendencies, or to punish them, is to create a severe conflict. Instead of conforming to our wishes, the dog will react decisively to prevent abnormal changes.

We like to believe we are superior to dogs. If that is so, we should not expect any dog to conform totally to our wishes. We must be the ones to adapt. After all, if we cannot accept a dog for what it is, how can we expect it to accept us?

We must examine each dog for its dominant and submissive tendencies. With this knowledge, we can learn to reinforce, rather than punish, its normal behavioral reactions. And we can learn to compromise to promote a positive relationship with the dog.

Table 1 lists a number of dominant and submissive behaviors commonly seen in dogs. Each dominant behavior has a submissive counterpart. In physics, every action has an equal and opposite reaction, and that is exactly what happens when a dominant dog and submissive dog interact. Dominant and submissive dogs do opposite things for the same reasons and similar things for opposite reasons. Check your dog's traits with those listed in this table to determine how dominant or submissive it is.

Dominant Dogs

The most dominant dogs are not house pets. Wolves, coyotes, and feral dogs live in wilderness areas away from people. They are too independent to look to people for help to survive. Less dominant dogs look to them for leadership because they behave in such a confident manner.

Dominant dogs mark territory with urine on a constant basis, but they are comfortable everywhere and roam great distances. They walk a straight line toward whatever they want. They prefer to hunt their own food, and go for a quick kill by biting the throat of their prey. They attack rather than back down when confronted by an intruder, although their purpose is usually to prove superiority rather than to kill. At night a dominant dog might be found atop a hill, howling to the moon as if to proclaim, "I'm king of the hill."

A truly dominant dog rarely makes a good house pet. It

Table 1: BEHAVIOR OPPOSITES

DOMINANT DOGS	SUBMISSIVE DOGS
Direct; quick action	Indirect; hesitant reaction
Leaders	Followers
Independent	Dependent
Confident, curious, arrogant	Fearful, self-doubting; may act guilty even when blameless
Large territory	Small territory
Comfortable anywhere	Comfortable only in center of home territory
Desire to be on top of things	Dig holes in ground; afraid of heights
Attack and chase off intruders	Run away from intruders or freeze in one spot
Try to escape confinement	Prefer confinement; afraid to explore new territory
Approach other animals and people	Desire center of attention; draw others toward them
Bite throat of other animal or person to kill	Bite only out of extreme fear; bite anything but the throat
Walk in straight lines	Walk in small circles; chase tails
Won't obey orders; give orders to others	Obey orders; cannot give orders
Refuse to behave like others	Mimic behavior of others
Hunt for food (predatory)	Beg and trade tricks for food; suck holes in materials
Gulp food	Nibble at food
Prefer fresh food	Eat stools of self or others
Chase cars	Car sickness; fear of cars
Bite others	Bite self (self-mutilation)
Lick other animals, people	Lick self
Soil house to mark territory	Soil house out of fear
Lift leg to urinate	Squat to urinate
Bark and howl for a reason (give orders, scare intruders, announce status, etc.)	Bark and howl out of fear of real or imagined dangers
Jump up on people	Roll over on back and expose belly to other people
Pull forward on leash	Strain backward on leash
Scratch and dig to get something specific	Scratch and dig out of frustration or fear

Try to act healthy even when sick	Sympathy lameness
Prefer balls, frisbees, round objects	Prefer leg bones and cylindrical objects
Protective of head and shoulders	Protective of paws and tails
Sexual mounting and pelvic thrusting	Accept sexual mounting by another; masturbation
Hyperaggression ?	Hyperactivity ?
More males than females	More females than males

refuses to obey orders or trade tricks for food, and does not tolerate long-term confinement. The most dominant pet dogs still retain many dominant tendencies, but their behavior is modified by more submissive tendencies then their wild counterparts possess.

Dominant pet dogs accept the dominance of a confident human leader. They actually prefer to look for a human leader rather than totally fend for themselves, but will not accept as a leader a person lacking self-confidence. This is especially important when arrogance from reproductive hormones replaces their natural confidence during mating seasons. A true human leader must respect the dominant dog's need to behave independently.

Dominant pet dogs do not roam as far as wild dogs. They tend to stay in their neighborhood rather than roam the countryside. Instead of climbing mountains, they may climb on furniture and their owners' laps. They may bark to order their owners to feed them, steal unprotected human food, or scratch and dig for garbage instead of hunting for live prey. They may gulp their food and guard their food bowl with their lives.

A dog shows its dominance to another dog by approaching from the side or rear, smelling its anal sacs (small sacs on each side of the anus which contain an aromatic material), then placing its front paws on the other dog's shoulders (Fig.1).Dogs distinguish one dog from another by the smell of the anal sac material, and they prove dominance by mounting other dogs. This dominance is typical, and is common between dogs and other animals and people. A highly dominant dog will attack

Fig. 1. Two dogs meet each other by smelling anal sac material located on each side of the anus.

and bite other dogs or people who try to mount it or put their front paws or hands on its shoulders.

Many people are unaware of a dog's vertical territorial needs, but a dog that jumps on our legs or laps is trying to proclaim its dominance over us. It appears to act like it is better than we are because it is higher up in the air. In extreme instances, a dog may actually knock a person down on all fours and then place its front paws on the person's shoulders, just like it would do to another dog (Figs. 2 and 3).

Some dominant male dogs force their owners to the floor to display dominance and also to ejaculate as if engaged in sexual activity. Sexual intercourse between two dogs actually is secondary to the act of dominance.

Fig. 2. Dogs that jump up on us are trying to dominate us.

Fig. 3. Some dogs are too dominant for some people.

Male dogs tend to be more dominant then females, at least during mating season. The male must dominate the female enough to invade her body with his. He must mount her and then thrust the pelvis back and forth. A dominant female will not allow a more submissive male to mount her, even if the male is not afraid to try. In these instances, successful reproduction is impossible and since successful matings generally perpetuate existing relationships, dominant males and submissive females continue to be born, although *some* males are not dominant and *some* females are not submissive. A female wolf is quite dominant compared with a female toy lap dog, but even some pet females display dominant tendencies.

Some female dogs mount other dogs and people just like males. Pelvic thrusting must also be part of the dominant instinct because females may show this behavior while perched on another dog's shoulders or a person's leg. Reproduction seems to be accidental when a male dog dominates a female dog during mating season, but the behaviors typical of the mating interaction are not just for reproduction (Fig. 4).

Since dominant dogs act like leaders, much of their behavior around people is to obtain and maintain leadership status. A dominant dog walks or runs in front of its owner. It pulls the owner toward a specific predetermined goal if it is on a leash.

Dominant dogs like to roam, especially during mating season. They feel an intense need to escape confinement and can quickly rush through open doors, jump over fences, break leash restraints, or scratch, dig, and chew to be free.

Since their territory is larger than the limits of their owners' property, dominant dogs feel compelled to check out and protect their entire territory. They cannot rest until all intruders and threats to their superiority have been expelled. Some dogs chase people on bicycles and pursue motor vehicles that pass through their territory. Many mailmen, meter readers, visitors, and overly friendly neighborhood children are bitten each year.

It is the dominant dog's nature to attack and scare off territorial intruders not recognized as friends. Dominant dogs are blamed for many bite wounds, but many times the injured person is at fault. In other cases, dog owners have failed to

Fig. 4. One dog dominates another by putting its paws on the other's shoulders. In this case, a neutered female is dominating an intact male.

understand their dogs' normal tendencies and have not either warned intruders or calmed their dogs.

Dominant dogs refuse to obey orders unless they have great respect for one special leader. In fact, they may respond to an order by doing exactly the opposite of what they are told to do, as if to prove that they alone have control over their own lives. While submissive, follower dogs may try to mimic the behavior of their leaders, dominant dogs seem to act differently from submissive dogs or less dominant people out of general principle. Dominant dogs also do not like to submit to disease or injury, and may try to continue daily activity when they should be resting.

The shape of objects in the environment may also affect dogs in different ways. Most dogs that are frisbie champions are dominant males. While it might be a generalization, it does appear that dominant dogs are attracted to round objects like balls and frisbies. Submissive dogs appear to be more attracted to leg bones and other cylindrical objects, and dislike or even fear round ones.

The terms "hyperaggression" and "hyperactivity" are also included in Table 1, but they are identified with question marks. Many people assume aggressiveness is limited to dominant dogs. It may just be a matter of semantics and confusion over definition, but many dog bite injuries are caused by nervous, submissive fear-biters. Many submissive dogs who are excessively frightened by all sights, sounds, and smells imagine threats to their survival. They may lash out and bite because of this real or imagined fear.

A condition known as hyperkinesis has been identified in both children and dogs. This syndrome is characterized by overactivity, distractibility, short attention span, impulsive activity, occasional aggression, and under-achievement despite normal intelligence. While hyperkinetic children and dogs seem to need medication to calm them, tranquilizers actually make the condition worse. Ironically, strong stimulants such as amphetamines work well to control hyperkinesis.

Scientists argue about the reasons for this seeming contradiction. It doesn't seem logical that hyperactivity might respond to a stimulant rather than a sedative. It makes sense though if hyperkinetic people are extremely submissive rather than dominant.

Perhaps hyperactivity comes from hypernervousness and, therefore, from submissiveness rather than dominance. Tranquilizers might make extremely insecure, fearful dogs more fearful and hyperactive because there is less self-control. Stimulants like amphetamines might give these dogs extra self-confidence, and hyperactive dogs might then perceive their environment more accurately and be less afraid. The stimulants might calm them down since they no longer fear every environmental change.

The causes of hyperaggression and hyperactivity must be

studied more fully. Dominant dogs are aggressive, but they do not usually kill, except for food. Territorial and mating squabbles between two dominant dogs rarely cause major injury to the fighters, since the confrontations are designed solely to gain dominance. Perhaps some hyperactive and hyperaggressive dogs are really fearful and submissive.

Submissive Dogs

The most submissive dogs behave exactly the opposite of the way dominant dogs do, but followers and leaders are attracted to one another. This dominant-submissive bond is quite similar to the attraction of opposite poles of a magnet. In magnetism, opposites attract and likes repel one another. It appears to be the same with dogs. Two equally dominant or equally submissive dogs often fight one another or remain separated.

Many people favor submissive dogs because they look to people for leadership. Followers require the assistance of a stronger leader in order to survive. They lack the confidence and dominant survival abilities to fend for themselves. Submissive dogs are so dependent, they are willing to sacrifice independent opportunities for the security, territory, food, and love that people can provide.

The most submissive dogs are afraid of almost everything. Whether real or imagined, they may fear every subtle change in their environment. This fear causes them to run away and hide. In the most extreme cases very submissive dogs may freeze in their tracks, unable to move. Instead of standing face to face with territorial intruders, submissive dogs turn around and face away, as if to prepare to escape.

The reflex responses of submissive dogs are predictable; they are almost always based on fear and self-doubt. They are afraid to obtain territory and feel secure only in the center of a small area. They prefer confinement to freedom, and they jump fences and dash through doors to return to their homes rather than escape from them.

Submissive dogs seem to have great difficulty walking a

straight line. If the only route toward food is a direct one, for example, a submissive dog may hesitate to fulfill its needs. Submissive dogs use circular patterns of movement. In fact, there appears to be a direct relationship between a dog's degree of dominance and the diameter of the circle it makes when it walks. The most submissive dogs walk in the smallest diameter circles, while dominant dogs walk in such large circles it appears they are moving in a straight line. A highly submissive dog may show spinning movements similar to tail chasing.

While dominant dogs seek vertical territory, submissive dogs are scared of height. These dogs are poor candidates for living in high-rise apartments because they may react fearfully to changes that would not frighten them on the ground. Submissive dogs tend to dig holes in the ground rather than climb on objects, as if they are trying to go down rather than up.

Because they are so fearful, submissive dogs cause many dog bite injuries. They bite out of intense fear, as if their lives are in constant jeopardy. Sudden movements, like children playing too roughly, may cause them to bite. However, since submissive dogs are not predatory and lack the confidence and directness to go for the enemy's head and throat, they generally bite a person's hands and feet (Figs. 5 and 6).

Submissive dogs claim so small a territory that they cannot independently satisfy many of their needs. They cannot capture food that is beyond the limits of their territory, so they must wait for food to come to them. If they do capture live prey, it is because the prey has stumbled into their territory. Many people are attracted to submissive dogs, and the dogs are quite successful at finding people who will bring them food every day.

Submissive dogs are successful beggars. Instead of obtaining their own food, they often try to trick their owners into feeding them. Many people believe a begging dog should be fed, and submissive dogs find begging consistent with their indirect approach to life. Many dogs learn quickly to beg more often than their nutritional needs require, perhaps as a device to get attention.

Submissive dogs often get food in exchange for performing

Fig. 5. A dominant dog may be an aggressive biter. It bares its teeth and lunges toward its target.

Fig. 6. A fear-biter growls and bares its teeth while backing away from the intruder to hide under a shelf.

tricks and obeying orders. The most trainable animals submit for their food, lodging, and love. Only dogs who are more submissive than their owners are trainable, since learning new behaviors requires a willingness to obey orders. While dominant dogs may behave just opposite to the way they are ordered, submissive dogs may learn to do almost anything to get a reward. They often mimic their owners' behaviors to demonstrate their subordinate, follower role.

Submissive dogs nibble slowly and rarely gulp their food. This is not a problem for single dogs, but families with two or more dogs might find that the more dominant dogs will gulp down their own food and then steal from the more submissive dogs. Since submissive dogs back off from a competitive challenge, they may go hungry without human intervention.

Submissive dogs have a tendency to suck holes in materials, especially woolens. This behavior might be an extension of newborn puppies' suckling instincts. While sucking wool is less common than some other behaviors, it is a possibility in any highly submissive dog.

On occasion, submissive dogs also eat their own stools or those of other animals. Several theories have been developed to explain this behavior called coprophagy. Possibly, submissive dogs are bored or are searching for added nutrition. In addition, submissive dogs display their subordinate role to more dominant dogs by eating their own waste deposits. Thus, coprophagy may be a normal submissive behavior for some dogs, and dogs confined to a small area, such as a cage or run, for extended periods of time, may show increasing tendencies for stool eating as self-confidence drops.

Submissive dogs strive to be the center of attention in their homes since they are so dependent and have so little personal territory. They often act uncomfortable when their owners ignore them or leave them alone for a long time. Since they lack self-confidence and shy away from independent activity, attention-getting is a means of increasing self-confidence by keeping the leader close by. This does not mean that owners should constantly cater to submissive dogs, but such dogs may act like they need frequent attention.

If a submissive dog craves attention, it will quickly learn what behaviors are successful. When a person responds to a certain behavior with love, food, or assistance, a submissive dog may repeat the behavior. If barking gets attention, the dog may continue to bark whether or not it needs anything. Submissive dogs seek attention by pretending to be lame or injured even when they are healthy, if their owners become concerned and run to them. Our emotional overreactions reinforce the pretending behavior of submissive dogs.

Real or imagined fear can result in many common submissive behaviors. In fact, fear causes these dogs to cower and act guilty even when they have done nothing wrong. If highly fearful, they may be unable to obey orders that are given in a loud tone of voice. The submissive dogs' fear may cause them to run and hide instead of complying. A submissive dog that fears many noises, sights, and sounds may spend a lot of time hiding under furniture or in a back corner of its home (Fig. 7).

Submissive dogs do not chase cars; they are afraid of motor vehicles and may even become sick when they must ride in one. When they bark and howl, it is often because of changes in their immediate environment, like thunderstorms and the presence of strange people or animals. They scratch and dig inside the home out of fear or frustration. Intense fear may cause a submissive dog to housesoil because it loses control and its body shakes.

Submissive dogs may crave close physical contact with people. They seem to be highly susceptible to our touch, and may depend on it to the extreme. In these cases, such a dog may become so content, it will fall over on its back when it is petted. It may enjoy this contact so much that it might prefer being touched rather than playing games or engaging in other activities.

A dog that is overly dependent on physical interrelationships may become self-destructive when such contact is absent. Dogs learn the value of touch from puppyhood because their mothers will fondle and lick them out of dominance, love, or both. Submissive dogs never seem to outgrow this need for physical contact. If they cannot get it from their owners, they may begin

18

Fig. 7. It is a submissive tendency that causes a dog to hide under furniture.

to lick, bite, and scratch themselves, as if they are trying to love themselves. Unfortunately, this behavior sometimes results in self-mutilation, since these dogs may not stop even when there is hair loss and physical irritation.

Submissive dogs may be too fearful to walk into new territory when placed on leash. While dominant dogs may try to pull their owners, submissive dogs on leashes may strain against such movement. They may have to be coaxed or dragged from the security of their home territories. Such behavior appears similar to that of a stubborn mule. Hyperactive, submissive dogs on leashes may appear to lunge in many different directions in reaction to various stimuli. They are not trying to run toward specific goals; rather, they are simply responding out of nervousness.

Most, but not all, submissive dogs are females. Most male dogs lift one leg to urinate, and most females squat. The tendency to squat is of submissive origin, but some females may lift a leg, and some males may squat.

Likewise, a female in heat often accepts the physical dominance of a male. She may allow him to mount her, place his paws on her shoulders, and engage her in sexual intercourse. Some male dogs are submissive enough to allow certain dominant males or females to mount them. Dominant dogs do not allow mounting and are especially protective of their heads and shoulders, while submissive dogs either accept mounting or roll over on their backs to expose their bellies (Fig. 8). Such dogs are more protective of their paws and rear end. Some submissive dogs engage in masturbation with or without sexual opportunities.

A Third Kind of Dog

Some dogs show mostly dominant behaviors, while others are primarily submissive. Many other dogs are mixtures of dominant and submissive traits and fall into a third category. These dogs may behave in a dominant fashion one minute and submissively the next. They are more unpredictable and vacillate more than either dominant or submissive dogs, but they are more adaptable and thus have greater potential to survive than either dominant or submissive dogs.

Dogs that are directly submissive and dogs that are indirectly dominant are included in this category. Some relatively dominant dogs appear willing to behave submissively for a particular purpose without losing confidence. These dogs are often easily obedience-trained. Directly submissive dogs may obey orders as an opportunity to share an experience with their masters instead of obeying orders out of fear or a need to follow. They may roll over and display their bellies as if submissive, but they do not lose confidence by doing so, and they may allow children and more submissive people to touch their shoulders and handle them roughly without reprisal.

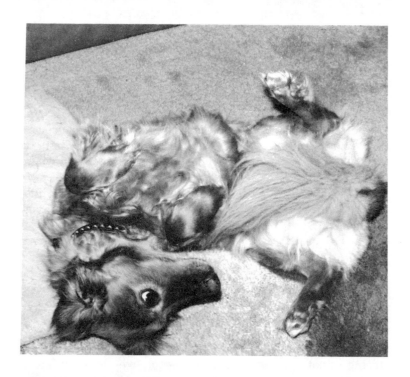

Fig. 8. Submissive dogs expose their bellies to dominant animals or people.

Indirectly dominant dogs have perspectives like submissive dogs. They claim a small home territory, prefer to be the center of attention, and are quite dependent. They do not use dominant instincts to fulfill their survival needs. They prefer an indirect approach, but they may exhibit dominant tendencies such as biting, destructive chewing, housesoiling, barking, and howling when others fail to fulfill their needs and wants. In essence, these dogs use dominant instincts secondarily as if for revenge. An indirectly dominant dog may enjoy being the center of attention so much that if its owner walks away, past the small limits of its psychological territory, it may bite at the person's legs. If the dog is spoiled and expects too much attention, it may respond negatively to anything that limits the owner's attention. If the owner must leave home for an extended period of time, the dog may respond by housesoiling or destructive chewing of furniture, the owner's clothes, etc. If the dog is accustomed to sleeping in bed with its owner, it may respond in similar fashion if it is suddenly locked out of the bedroom.

Indirectly dominant dogs often make fine pets because they are not natural leaders, and they lack the fear that limits the activity of highly submissive dogs. However, if their owners fail to provide consistent leadership, these dogs are often good candidates for behavior problems. Under these conditions, indirectly dominant dogs are quick to act like leaders in the home, even though they may not know how to lead.

These dogs may expect their owners to pick them up, to carry them, or put them on their laps, but they may act like they are in charge of the owners once placed in a position of dominance. The indirect tricks they use to gain dominance are considered cute by many people, and they often find it easy to gain control over their owners. If a person notices these tricks and refuses to submit to such a dog's whims, the dog may pout, glare, hide under a table, or even bite the owner. Revenge biting is not aggressiveness, but people who lack confidence may unknowingly encourage this biting by their fear of reprisals.

Indirectly dominant dogs may like to give orders, but these orders seem to come from a perspective different from that of dominant dogs. Truly dominant dogs give orders to restrict the activity of other dogs or people. They behave in a dominant fashion to say things like, "Leave me alone," "Don't do this," "Don't do that," "Step aside for the leader." On the other hand, indirectly dominant dogs order others to get them things. They may act like they expect others to "Get me food," "Pet me," "Put me on a pedestal."

Indirectly dominant dogs may be self-destructive if their owners fail to recognize that they are followers rather than leaders. These dogs are easily spoiled by permissiveness. If people continue to give in to attention-getting tricks, such dogs may begin to expect more attention and indirect dominance than they really need to survive. A vicious cycle ensues, because the more we give, the more they expect.

Some indirectly dominant dogs can only be described as sneaky. They may know what their owners do not permit, but they may comply only when their owners are watching. They may wait until the owners are away or asleep to do those things they cannot do in the owner's presence. Indirectly dominant dogs are commonly sneaky and ingenious.

Like spoiled children, they may act like the boss in their own homes. Since they are not confident leaders, though, they become quite nervous if allowed to gain too much dominance. Despite their attempts to the contrary, indirectly dominant dogs really need to follow more confident leaders. If allowed to lead, they make incorrect decisions which could harm themselves and their owners. Indirectly dominant dogs often appreciate simple forms of punishment. A quick backhand to the muzzle has the same meaning as their mother putting them in their place with a paw slap. They seem to appreciate the opportunity to follow rather than lead.

Some of the most confident dogs, the most natural leaders, are mixtures of dominant and submissive. A dog that can utilize either dominant or submissive instincts at the correct time to maximize its chance to survive has more self-confidence than other dogs. A dominant dog may gain confidence when it wins a competition, but, when it loses because it has difficulty accepting a submissive role, its confidence may be shattered. A submissive dog may gain some confidence when indirect methods help fulfill its needs, but it may be too afraid to use a dominant technique even when it has no choice. The dog that uses dominance when it should submit and submissiveness when it should dominate loses self-confidence with every loss.

The most confident dogs have learned through experience that they can use both dominant and submissive instincts to maximize their survival. Every successful interaction increases confidence, and they have many opportunities for success. These dogs are so confident that they act as if they have no reason to prove their superiority to others. This confident air is so appealing that other dogs are often eager to follow.

The dominant-submissive relationship can be demonstrated as a seesaw or as a legal scale. Dominant dogs with few submissive instincts tip the scales to one side, and submissive dogs with few dominant instincts tip the scales to the other. Dogs with equal mixtures of dominant and submissive keep the scales balanced and have the greatest chance to survive.

The dominant-submissive relationship in any dog is a dynamic one, and an alternation between the two is necessary. A simple game of "fetch" is a good example: A dog leaves the owner's side to chase down and dominate a stick well enough to pick it up, and then returns to the owner. This back-and-forth movement requires both a dominant instinct to leave the owner, and a submissive instinct to return to the owner.

A dog develops an increasing need to use an opposite behavior in order to reachieve a balance when it is permitted or forced to move too far to one end of these scales. "Explosions" of behavior in dogs often come from prolonged inability to regularly use these behavioral opposites. A highly dominant dog may suddenly lose self-control and hallucinate to counteract prolonged dominance. A highly submissive dog may suddenly become a fear-biter or eat excessively to utilize dominant instincts that are not utilized in other ways.

Dogs that are forced to submit or are permitted to dominate too much will eventually utilize an opposite behavior to reestablish a natural balance. The more a dog is pushed in one direction, the stronger the opposite reaction is going to be.

No two dogs are exactly alike, because they are all mixtures of dominant and submissive. The possible combinations of these mixtures are too numerous to count. As dog owners, we should observe each dog individually to gain an understanding of its natural tendencies. We can compare our findings with Table 1. Once we understand our dogs, we can then adapt our own behaviors to enhance, rather than limit, our dogs' chances for survival and, therefore, their behavioral contentment.

The Senses

It is important to understand a dog's sensing abilities because it cannot use its instincts unless it can perceive changes in its environment. A dog uses the senses of sight, hearing, smell, taste, and touch with great success. There is definite evidence to support the idea of a sixth sense similar to extra sensory perception (ESP) or mental telepathy. Sensing ability is often more highly developed in dogs than in humans.

Dogs supposedly see less detail than humans do during daylight, but they see better than people do in darkness. While they may not be able to see from great distances, dogs can see some things quite clearly. They easily recognize sudden movements and changes in light intensity. Of course, a dog's reaction to these sudden changes depends on its degree of confidence. A fearful dog may run away from sudden movements, such as a child's arm rushing toward its head.

Confident dogs have more useful visual abilities than either fearful or arrogant dogs. Fearful dogs do not appear to focus on objects outside their small psychological territory. They are afraid to explore new territory, perhaps because they cannot see what is out there. Of course, they may turn away from an object outside the territory before they can focus well enough to see what it is, because they are afraid. Another theory holds that perhaps their eyes deceive them and cause them unnecessary fear by distorting and enlarging their environment, making it appear more threatening than it really is. Arrogant dogs sometimes act as if they can go wherever they wish, and run into things because they don't pay attention to where they are going.

Confident dogs may stare intently at objects that pass, and follow each movement precisely. It is difficult to say how well they actually can see, but some of these dogs seem to base many of their responses primarily on sight. This is in contrast to the majority of dogs that use sight only to supplement their other senses. Most blind dogs have no trouble maneuvering around obstacles in their homes because their other senses make up for their lack of sight.

Dogs have a highly-developed sense of smell. It is believed that dogs can smell thousands of times better than humans. Their noses and brains have more smell sensors than we have, but dogs also have a vomeronasal gland in the back of their throats which is absent in people. Dogs smell both by sniffing and by opening their mouths. This is mainly why male dogs know when there's a female in heat in the neighborhood, and how a dog inside a closed house might know when another animal is urinating or defecating in its yard even though its owners cannot understand why the dog is trying to go outside.

Think about what this means. A small bit of perfume might smell like a whole perfume factory to a dog. Dinner cooking on the stove might be a huge, if not irresistible, temptation. A teenager reaching puberty may be more recognizable to a dog than to a person. A dog may recognize our present positive or negative attitudes and confidence levels by even our most subtle body odors. Some dogs make great hunters and trackers, and can follow a scent for many miles. Even nonhunters are much more affected by smells in their environment than we can possibly appreciate.

Dogs also have a highly developed ability to hear. If a dog is afraid of unusual or unpredictable noises, it may bark, hide, or show other nervous reactions to outside sounds that we do not recognize. We shouldn't blame our dogs for their responses just because we may not hear the same noises. A confident dog probably tunes out most noises, but a fearful dog may always be hyperactive and jumpy in metropolitan areas that are very noisy. This is especially true if a dog perceives these noises as real or imagined threats.

Fearful dogs run away from loud noises, but highly dominant dogs may seek to compete against their source. This competition may take the form of an attack in extreme cases, but more commonly, a dominant dog howls to the moon, then howls louder after being yelled at to quiet down. The louder the owner yells, the louder the dog's response. Such a dog may quiet down more quickly if the owner lets it complete its howling or says "Good dog" to submit to its need to shout out.

Like the sense of smell, dogs have a much stronger sense of hearing than people do. To a dog, living in an environment with many sounds or smells is probably equivalent to a person with perfect pitch listening to a grade school orchestra concert. We should be much more tolerant of dogs that react adversely to the sounds and smells in their environment, since these strong sensing devices help dogs survive in a hectic, highly competitive world.

There is much evidence to support the notion of a "sixth sense." Perhaps our ignorance or lack of sufficient scientific research causes us to examine such a notion. Perhaps instead of an extra sense, dogs have a mysterious but advantageous insight when they combine the use of their five recognized senses. Maybe this insight comes from an interaction of electromagnetic auras. Whatever the reason, some dogs have been known to travel hundreds of miles to find their owners or return to a previous home. Some dogs can perceive disasters like earthquakes, storms, and fires before they happen, and some seem to react specifically to our thoughts even before we relate them verbally or physically.

In addition, all dogs sense our attitudes and confidence levels almost instantaneously. They see our body language, hear our voice inflections, and smell our body odors, but each of these situations requires a small time delay between a dog's recognition of sights, sounds, and smells, and its response. It seems like dogs can sense our emotional and attitudinal changes quicker than that.

For example, many people, upon returning home, have noticed their dogs may act guilty, as if they know they have done something wrong. Most behaviorists believe dogs have too short a memory to remember some episode that occurred while their owners were gone. It appears that dogs "act guilty" by cowering to the threat posed by a negative attitude toward them. A common finding in these cases is that the people anticipated problems upon entering the door because they remembered yesterday's problems. Their anticipation led to a negative, threatening attitude that their dogs sensed immediately.

Dogs have no choice but to behave as their instincts dictate. They must fulfill the basic needs for food, territory, reproduction, protection, and love, and their instincts help ensure their survival. When we punish or blame dogs for following their natural instincts, we keep them from fulfilling their survival needs. Every time a dog successfully completes an instinctive reaction, self-confidence increases and helps a dog maintain its will to live. Every time a dog fails to fulfill its basic needs in its own way, it loses confidence. If that happens too much, it loses the will to live and it dies.

All dogs are totally selfish until their basic needs are fulfilled. A dominant dog is selfish in a direct way, and a submissive dog is selfish in an indirect way, but they are both equally selfish. Dogs compromise enough to share a life with their owners only when their basic needs are fulfilled. Most people can achieve all the rewards of pet ownership, such as sharing love and closeness with most dogs. But first we must understand them well enough to help them be themselves and fulfill their basic survival needs.

Chapter 3

EARLY BEHAVIOR DEVELOPMENT

While a dog's nervous system and its full set of abilities and behavioral tendencies are not completely developed until several weeks or months after birth, discussions of early behavior development should begin at least at the time of birth, if not at conception.

It is now known that a bitch instinctively submits to hormonal "orders" from her unborn pups. These pups involuntarily send hormones to their mother's brain to help regulate food intake and nutritional balance. While developing fetuses remain content within the security of the womb for some time, they develop an increasing need to escape the womb and the water bag in which they reside. When birth is near, fetal hormones "order" the mother to begin the uterine and abdominal contractions necessary to help the pups make their final escape from the womb.

The bitch uses both dominant and submissive instincts when she is pregnant. She submits to hormonal orders for food and birth and perhaps much more, but she also dominates the pups by holding them within her uterus until whelping is near. Just prior to whelping, the bitch actively seeks a secluded, dark, warm area and builds a "nest" out of papers, blankets, and similar materials at her disposal. She becomes less responsive to commands from her owners as she becomes more committed to the needs of her pups. She may begin to carry around (dominate) toys and other objects as if she is mothering them.

Birth is an important event for a puppy because successful completion of its escape attempt gives it a strong initial boost in survival confidence. This need to escape confinement and the water bag may be especially strong for dominant dogs that continue to dislike both confinement and bathing throughout their lives.

The mother eats the afterbirth, bites off the umbilical cord, and licks the puppy from head to tail, thus showing a dominant instinct. The licking stimulates breathing and defecation, but it may also be perceived as an act of love, for the puppy submits to this dominance and moves toward the mother to nurse. Puppies are usually born with a strong sucking reflex as well as a need for the warmth and security of the mother's body. The sucking dominates the nipples while the pup is submitting simultaneously to its need for love, security, and nourishment.

For the first two to three weeks after birth, puppies do little besides eat and sleep. When they are hungry, they cry for food and thereby induce a hormone in the mother called oxytocin, which stimulates milk production. In essence, a crying puppy is ordering its mother to produce milk.

While many behavior traits have not yet developed, it appears that even from birth, dominant pups successfully compete for milk against their submissive littermates. These pups are more aggressive at reaching and monopolizing the milk supply, especially the posterior breasts that produce the most milk. Submissive pups may be prevented from obtaining as much nourishment if the litter is large or the milk supply short.

Dominant and submissive behaviors become more obvious at around three weeks of age, as a litter of puppies establishes its own "pecking order." The more independent and aggressive pups begin to display dominance over their more fearful littermates in ways other than food procurement. A dominant pup walks proudly with head and tail up and ears erect. It ignores its littermates except to dominate them or compete for territory. It begins to smell the rear end of more submissive pups and to mount from the side to place its paws on their shoulders.

Submissive pups either accept this dominance or roll over to expose their bellies. As they walk around, their ears may remain down, with their heads lowered and eyes directed toward the ground. Their tails may be curled between their hind legs, especially when they turn or run away out of fear. The way a pup orients itself relative to its littermates at three weeks of age is a good indication of the natural tendencies which will continue throughout its life.

The more dominant pups begin to leave the security of the mother and whelping area to explore new territory. They use a dominant instinct to do this, but it is a submissive instinct that causes them to return each time to their mother. Their lives constantly alternate between dominant and submissive instincts.

A dominant pup may emphasize escape over return, while a submissive pup's behavior is exactly opposite. A good mother helps balance these extremes for the ultimate benefit of all the pups. If a puppy moves too far from the mother, she goes after it and may hit it with her paw and either herd or mouth-carry it back to the whelping area. This helps keep it from encountering dangers before it can handle them. Mothers are often extremely possessive of newborn pups (Fig. 9).

A pup that is overly submissive may be too dependent on the mother for its own good, and the bitch may try to force it to be more independent by pushing it away from her with her nose or paws. Or she may roll over onto her stomach to prevent nursing, or simply leave the nesting area for awhile.

Both sets of motherly responses are considered acts of love that ultimately improve a pup's survival chances. Not even a dominant puppy can totally fend for itself prior to weaning. Motherly dominance reminds it of its own limitations without excess suffering. But no puppy can live long if it is totally dependent on its mother for survival. The mother cannot and will not always be there to fulfill its needs, and survival depends at least partially on the confidence gained from independent action. The mother's opposite approach to her dominant and submissive puppies helps them balance both sets of instinctive needs.

Pups learn to develop their own instinctive tendencies by observing their mother and other adult dogs as well as by playing with their littermates. Each interaction between mother and pup is a learning experience, helping attune a pup to its own nature and develop its instincts through repetition. Adult dogs "teach" puppies by example, so pups learn to mimic advantageous behaviors such as those used for hunting and reproduction. Puppies often learn most from their mistakes; a pup lacking in experiences has few learning opportunities.

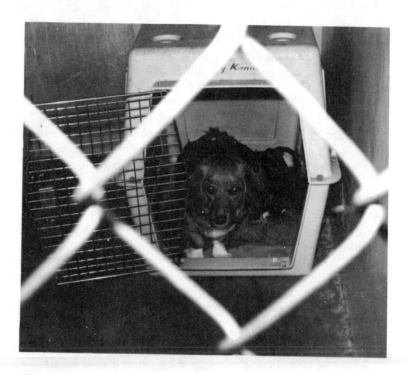

Fig. 9. Mothers are often quite protective of their pups.

Play time is a chance to practice instincts and make mistakes. Behaviors demonstrated during play are the same ones puppies will use to fulfill specific survival needs later in their lives. In addition to the hierarchy development described earlier, play behavior also includes sexual mounting, attention-getting, and hunting activities such as stalking and pouncing.

Play-fighting serves an important function. Puppies learn how to protect themselves during play-fighting, and how to interact favorably with other animals and people. In fact, the feedback pups gain from other pups during fighting helps to moderate behavioral extremes.

Most play-fighting between puppies is mild and is not designed to cause injury. If one puppy becomes too dominant and bites another puppy hard enough to cause pain, though, the second puppy may bite back. Such negative reinforcement appears to prevent the dominant puppy from wanting to repeat its behavior. It learns to gain dominance by more subtle means than actual aggressiveness. In contrast, a puppy raised in isolation from its mother and littermates may not learn to control its mouthing tendencies and may become a too-aggressive biter as an adult.

Submissive dogs can also learn during play-fighting. They may learn to prevent actual fights later in life by displaying submissive postures. These postures tell a dominant dog it does not have to fight to prove its superiority. This may actually improve a submissive's pup's confidence. It actually wins by pretending to be a loser, preventing the confrontation that would otherwise ensue. Sometimes during play, a more dominant dog may permit a submissive dog to dominate temporarily. Such action helps reinforce the opposite set of tendencies in both dogs, helping them maintain a balance and preventing extremes.

Research of several animal species including dogs indicates that pups truly need interactions with other dogs during their early development. A pup raised in total isolation from three weeks of age may suffer from a poorly developed nervous system. It appears that an absence of physical and emotional closeness specifically inhibits normal development of the central nervous system. Such dogs adjust poorly to real-life situations and may have shorter lifespans.

Pups forced to grow up isolated from other dogs may become poorly socialized and have difficulty relating to other dogs, animals, and people. This is especially true if the people caring for them provide only the bare essentials and do not play with them or interact physically. Such dogs may become overly dependent on their caretakers. They learn only a submissive role rather than how to interact using both dominant and submissive instincts, and they may become highly introverted and asocial as adults.

Social isolation may cause confusion regarding a dog's sexual behavior. Dogs that have no contact with other dogs at an early age may, as adults, have difficulty interacting sexually. They may even show sexual preferences for the animal species they interacted with as pups. If the only interpersonal contact pups receive at an early age is with people, they may regard themselves as people and may prefer people over dogs as sexual partners.

Weaning is a natural process that occurs around six weeks of age, although this may vary considerably. Weaning is a time when puppies and their mothers make a final, complete break from one another. The mother may need to display her dominance more specifically, since she has had to submit so frequently to the needs of her pups. The pups reach a point where they also must display their dominance and escape the mother. Otherwise, there would be excessive competition for survival needs between mother and offspring.

Some mothers may wean earlier than six weeks, especially if they have strong dominant instincts. They require their own independence again and tire of their nipples being chewed by their pups' sharp teeth. If they are too dominant, these mothers may push their pups from the nest before they are ready to leave. Worse, they may kill the pups or refuse to let them nurse.

Highly submissive mothers may try to hold onto their offspring longer than necessary. They seem to enjoy their dependent role and fear the loss of their puppies. They may actually force them to leave the nest by trying to hold onto them.

The actual time of weaning, then, depends on both mother and pups, when both feel a need to escape each other. Puppies feel such a strong need to escape that they suddenly can no longer tolerate mother's milk. If forced to drink it after weaning, pups will vomit. They must escape the mother both externally and internally.

Final weaning is so complete that a dominant male puppy may never be able to mate sexually with its mother. It appears that the male pup desires so much to escape its mother's womb that it cannot return to it, even partially, to complete the sexual act. Female pups may ultimately mate with their fathers, but perhaps never with male littermates.

The successful completion of weaning gives a pup another

big boost in survival confidence, if weaning occurs at the proper time. A pup may become excessively fearful or aggressive if weaned too early or too late (Fig. 10). Leaving the mother reinforces the dominant instinct a dog needs to fend for itself, while reducing its need for dependent security. The completion of weaning is also beneficial for the mother, since it improves her own survival confidence and prepares her for the next mating season.

Weaning is the best time to introduce a puppy to a human home. A dominant puppy may develop so much self-confidence in the few weeks after weaning that it becomes too independent to make a good pet. Placing a dominant pup in a home with human leaders right after weaning helps prevent it from becoming too independent.

Fig. 10. Puppies weaned and isolated at too young an age may become overly fearful.

A submissive pup fears drastic changes in its environment, and weaning can make it excessively nervous and emotionally upset. Placing a submissive pup in a good home right after weaning helps it retain its self-confidence if its new leaders give it the care and reassurance it needs. A negative home environment, of course, can be traumatic for any puppy.

While pups can learn to interact positively with people anytime between three and fourteen weeks of age, the optimum time for socialization is six to eight weeks. At this age, we have the best chance to domesticate (tame) puppies to accept us as their leaders. We actually replace a puppy's mother in its life, and maintain the relationship to which it is accustomed.

Meaningful handling from people willing to play the role of mother encourages a six- to eight-week-old puppy to become somewhat dependent: it is necessary to prevent total independence if we want the pup to obey our orders and live as a family member in a home. In the proper human and dog relationship, the person plays the role of a strong, protective leader, setting necessary limits while providing constant love, praise, and reassurance for every positive behavior, no matter how insignificant. Pups are most willing to transfer allegiance from a mother to a person when they are six to eight weeks old.

A pup should interact meaningfully with happy, confident, loving people on a daily basis by the time it is six weeks of age, whether it is placed in a home or continues to live with a breeder, or in a kennel or pet store. It should not be handled constantly, just consistently and with a purpose. This improves a pup's ability to accept a strange home and to accept humans as secure authority figures.

There is a major difference between *meaningful* handling and *frequent* handling. All dogs need some physical contact, and they need to learn to submit to dominant handling by people. But a dominant dog handled too much will rebel, and a submissive dog will become overly dependent. Some people seem to hold their dogs for long periods of time, and while this may fulfill our own need for warmth and closeness, it gives a submissive dog too few opportunities to reinforce its independent, dominant tendencies. Such a dog may become overdependent, and too fearful to leave its owner's grasp.

If a pup is not able to enjoy human security by the time it is eight to ten weeks old, the so-called "fear imprint" stage can produce permanently negative psychological effects. Submissive pups in any stressful situation, and those isolated in cages through ten weeks of age, can develop intense fears. The cage is their only security, and it lacks warmth and love. Whatever specific frightening changes occur in the pup's life at this time may remain a permanent part of its memory, and it may overreact to any future stimulus that even remotely resembles its previous frightening experience.

Even puppies that are socialized into good homes before they are eight weeks old can suffer from fear—imprinting at eight to ten weeks. If a child unknowingly scares and hurts a puppy by hitting it or jumping toward it too fast, the pup can grow into an adult dog that runs away or bites whenever someone makes a sudden move toward it. Any change that occurs at eight to ten weeks, no matter how subtle, can be negatively imprinted in a pup's memory.

Sexual maturity begins when a pup is six to twelve months of age, but meaningful sexual mounting behaviors can begin as early as twelve to fourteen weeks. All dogs have areas of special sensitivity on their bodies which they like to rub or have touched. At even this early age, a puppy becomes aware of the shoulders, neck, chin, chest, lower abdomen, nipples, rear end, and genitals, and it quickly learns ways of satisfying its need for tactile stimulation. Male dogs also begin to have erections at this time.

Barking at strangers and territorial intruders begins as early as eighteen weeks of age in some dogs, and no later than one year of age in others. Males also begin to leg-lift at this time. If a pup receives continuous reinforcement of its aggressive territorial tendencies at this age, it may begin to behave this way all the time. Every successful attempt at domination becomes its own reward and encourages behavioral repetition. Once a dog is about two, such behavior becomes difficult to modify because the dog has developed too much confidence in its dominant tendencies.

By the time a dog reaches maturity, it has developed specific, highly recognizable behavior patterns. It will use its fight or flight reflex for every change in its environment or lifestyle. If the environment is stable, the dog may behave predictably and within acceptable limits throughout its life. A dog that satisfies both its dominant leader and submissive security needs will be emotionally content and physically healthy.

The Role of Heredity and Natural Selection

Some psychologists believe that environment alone influences behavior. This theory holds that if you change the environment, you change a dog's behavior. This is partially true, but environment alone cannot make a highly fearful dog dominant or change a highly confident dog into a submissive one. Within limits, we can modify a dog's behavior by modifying its environment, but we cannot totally change a dog's behavior to fit our whims. Heredity contributes a great deal to a dog's natural tendencies.

Even people who do not support theories of genetics and heredity agree that physical characteristics are passed on from generation to generation through reproduction. It seem illogical that behavior would be independent of hereditary factors. A mating between two dominant wolves produces another dominant wolf and not a submissive lap dog that happens to look like a wolf.

To analyze a pup's behavior, one should begin by examining the natural tendencies of its mother and father since it is a genetic mixture of both parents. If a pup's parents create behavior problems for their owners, there is a strong likelihood that their pup will have similar problems around similar people. Dog breeders mate males and females that can pass along physical characteristics show judges prefer, but they sometimes overlook behavioral considerations. Perhaps this is why highly inbred dogs have a greater tendency to have psychological disorders.

Each dog breed has certain behavioral tendencies and instinctive capabilities which makes it valuable to people. Hunting dogs have a natural ability to assist people in their hunting. Some follow a scent, some flush or point to a prey, some retrieve killed prey. These abilities are passed from generation to generation by heredity, and they are reinforced and enhanced through repetition, reinforcement, and training. Such behaviors cannot be taught to dogs that were born without these hereditary tendencies.

Dogs born with certain special behavioral traits must utilize these abilities whether they are trained to do so or not. Dachshunds are initially bred to follow badgers into their burrows. Their long noses, long bodies, and short legs facilitate movement through long, narrow tunnels in the ground. While most dachshunds are no longer used for this purpose, they may still need to root and dig the ground and explore holes in the ground even without badgers nearby. The person who punishes a dachshund for this behavior goes against its nature.

The most popular purebred dogs suffer greatly from excessive inbreeding. A champion male is often bred with numerous females of the same breed and later with his own daughters. While the idea of perpetuating the sire's championship physical characteristics sounds good, inbreeding is a one-way street which ultimately leads to many problems. These breeds suffer from a large number of hereditary physical defects. Some of them are psychotic or neurotic, suffer from emotional instability, and have behavior problems.

Mixed-breed dogs have many advantages over purebred dogs because they have more genetic variability. Mixtures of physical and behavioral characteristics prevent the predominance of weaknesses commonly found in dogs with a small number of genetic options. Breeding two highly submissive dogs can only result in submissive offspring, but mixing dominant and submissive traits gives offspring a wider range of behaviors with which to adapt more readily to changes in the environment. Generally, mixed-breed dogs are healthier and more behaviorally adaptable than purebred dogs.

Many people misunderstand the phrase "survival of the fittest." They imagine that in nature, the strong survive and the weak perish. However, "fitness" comes from adaptability rather than physical strength. Dogs that have the ability to use both dominant and submissive instincts, and to use them at the proper times, have a far greater chance of survival than dogs with only dominant or submissive abilities.

It is impossible for a dog to survive if it is totally dominant or totally submissive. A totally dominant dog is not as "fit" as one might expect. Its self-confidence is actually arrogance, since it imagines itself to be king of the world. This arrogance is as self-destructive as fear because such a dog cannot respect any of nature's strengths. This dog, because it is arrogant, might jump right into an animal trap because it doesn't hesitate long enough to know where it is going. It might try to defy a thunderstorm by standing in a puddle of water and howling at it as lightning strikes and kills it. It might fail to seek help even when it cannot live without assistance. It might attack a person who likes nothing better than to kill aggressive dogs. A dominant dog cannot live long without a few submissive instincts to modify its arrogance.

A totally submissive dog cannot live long, either. If it is too fearful to help itself in any way, it will be destroyed. It might freeze in its tracks in the middle of the road at the sight of an approaching car, and be run over. If it is totally dependent on another animal or person, it will suffer when that assistance is absent. Its fear of everything will be so stressful that the dog will pick up any stray disease. It will mutilate itself to death, or be too afraid to eat foods it must have to survive. While many of us feel sorry for these animals and try to protect and care for them, no person is totally unselfish and reliable twenty-four hours a day, and cannot totally save submissive dogs from self-destruction.

Many centuries ago, pet dogs were wild animals that befriended humans. They had to have been among the most dependent wild dogs to do this, and they discovered they could improve their survival chances by teaming up with people. Thus, pet dogs began with a number of submissive tendencies. The most dominant dogs would never have submitted to people in the first place.

Through the years, we have interfered with dog breeding to produce offspring that can help fulfill our own needs. We favor dependent, submissive dogs, and that has reduced the number of dominant behaviors possible in our dogs. Now, many centuries later, we have helped to create new dog breeds that cannot possibly live on their own without human assistance. This is unfortunate, because in trying to help dogs secondarily to them helping us, we now have dogs whose lives depend on people who do not understand them completely.

Through evolution, pet dogs have become weaker and more dependent and submissive. Dogs have more physical and emotional problems than ever before. There are some breeds that may be relatively close to extinction because we have not learned enough about the importance of genetics. Without genetic variability, many dogs may reach a point where they can no longer live within our complex society.

If we are to reverse this trend for the betterment of all dogs, we must learn much more about dogs. We must learn to understand their needs and help them to satisfy them *before* we can expect them to fulfill ours. If not, our selfishness may backfire completely.

Chapter 4

CANINE COMMUNICATION METHODS

Communication between two people is said to be 55 percent body language, 38 percent voice intonation, and only 7 percent verbal. The actual words we use are less important than the impressions we give off with our bodies and tone of voice. Body movements most accurately reflect our true thoughts.

Dogs do not use words to communicate; they have no need for them. Unless dogs are too fearful or arrogant to carefully observe their environment, most can tell what we are thinking by watching our body movements. Dogs use many different body postures to communicate with each other, and they interpret human body postures in the same way. We can also understand our dogs better by observing their actions.

Humans tend to rely a great deal on words, but most dogs do not have this problem. They are perhaps fortunate because they are less likely to accept the nontruths people sometimes express verbally. To survive, dogs must accurately interpret their environment, and body language is far more precise than verbal language.

When a dog jumps up and down at the front door, we don't need a translator to tell us it wants to go outside. When it lifts one rear leg, we know it is going to urinate. When a dog chases a moving automobile, it is most probably trying to run the car off its territory. These are overt behaviors that are easy to interpret, but many more subtle clues can be recognized if we observe a dog's behavior closely. We need to interpret these behaviors accurately so that we will not misinterpret and be in conflict with a dog's real needs.

Some people allow their dogs to jump up on their legs or laps because they believe their dogs are happy to see them and are expressing their love. They may be happy to see us, but dogs jump up on people to dominate them the same way they would other dogs. A dog that jumps up on a person's lap is obtaining vertical territory, as if to demonstrate superiority.

Lap-sitting may be mutually beneficial to both the dog and its owner, but to permit this behavior at all times reinforces the dog's dominant instincts, and the dog might become more aggressive to demonstrate its dominance in other ways. This is a common result of the owner's failure to recognize the truth behind the behavior.

Referring again to Table 1, every dominant and submissive tendency tells us how a dog perceives itself relative to its environment. A truly aggressive, dominant dog maintains direct eye contact with anyone approaching its psychological territory. Its body language demonstrates classic signs of pride and dominance: erect body posture with forward leaning, ears erect and forward or outward and downward, tail elevated with the tip moved forcefully back and forth, and lips curled with teeth displayed. The head is raised with the neck arched, all four legs are extended stiffly, and hair on the shoulders and rear stand on end, all making the dog appear larger and more threatening. It utters a low, throaty growl as it poises for attack. It is especially sensitive to any attempt to dominate its head and shoulders.

Inside a cage or other small, confined area, a dominant dog stands on its hind legs against the door, growls at passersby, and bites and scratches to break down the barrier that restrains it (Fig. 11). Even leash restraint causes anger, and encourages viciousness for dogs undergoing attack training. Dominant dogs need more territory, not less, and their actions tell us so.

On the other hand, a submissive dog sees a cage as a source of security. When it is afraid, it cowers and shakes in a back corner of the cage. Its ears are pushed backwards against its head, the tail is between the legs, the eyes are turned downward and away, and the back is arched. It may raise a front paw as if to defend itself. If it is a fear-biter, it may show its teeth and growl, but it does so as it draws its head away rather than toward the threat. Despite the aggressive facial expression, its trembling body posture tells us it is fearful rather than dominant (Fig. 12).

Indirectly dominant dogs are often quite expressive, especially when they do not get their way. Their body language in

Fig. 11. Dominant dogs need more territory.

these instances is quite similar to that of spoiled children. They may pout, snort, whimper, or even glare at the owner or object of disgust. They may walk away with their tails between their legs and may seek seclusion in a back room or under a bed, table, or other piece of furniture. They may show their frustration by chewing or tearing clothes, bedsheets, or other objects, especially those belonging to the person who resisted their submissive attempts at dominance. Revenge biting and nonaggressive growling are also possible.

A happy, contented dog is easy to distinguish. It may literally plop down on the floor as if jumping at the chance to relax. It may roll over to rub its back on the floor, swaying its head and rear end back and forth. It shows no fear but also total disregard about fulfilling any of its survival needs. It will sleep soundly

Fig. 12. A fearful dog backs itself into corners and shakes fearfully.

through distracting noises, perhaps only lifting one ear in a half-hearted attempt to determine their source. It may sleep either in a curled-up position or stretched out straight. It may dream during sleep, and uncontrolled barking sounds and periodic leg movements may mean it is dreaming of its favorite exercise or activity.

When a dog wants to play or to make up with its owner after it has been disciplined, it may slowly crawl forward toward the owner with its body close to the ground, its rear end elevated slightly, and its tail wagging back and forth. If it wants to play, the dog may paw the ground and pounce playfully at imaginary objects. It acts excited but tentative, and waits for a positive response.

Play, and many other behaviors, are most likely to occur in dogs with relatively equal mixtures of dominant and submissive tendencies. Such dogs can behave in ways too complex for the scope of this book. Ideally, we should closely examine each dog for its unique combination of body movements. Once we have correctly associated a certain facial expression and body posture with a specific attitude, we can better distinguish the subtle changes which might indicate a different attitude.

Body language is extremely important in communication, but dogs have many ways of communicating with us. Voice intonation is important, too. Dogs use many different sounds in an effort to communicate. Basenjis are known as "barkless" dogs, but even they have vocal cords and can growl and shriek when necessary. Dogs appear to understand each other's barking sound, and with practice, we can learn the true nature of many of these sounds.

Dogs vary the pitch, intensity, and frequency of vocal sounds. High-pitched, soft sounds are submissive, and deep, loud sounds are dominant. A submissive toy dog's deepest sounds may be higher pitched than a dominant wolf's highest pitched sounds. Every dog that can vocalize at all has a range of pitches to fulfill both dominant and submissive needs.

Dogs vocalize to announce their presence or their status, to demonstrate frustration, pain, or disgust, to get attention or cry for help, to scare off intruders, and to compete against other noises. Fearful dogs may bark incessantly with no apparent purpose other than as a nervous reaction to fear—inducing stimuli. Dominant dogs may bark louder when their owners yell at them to stop barking.

When a dog makes noises, try to determine why, and listen for subtle differences in voice intonation. All forms of barking may sound similar to the untrained ear, but a dog's attempts at vocalization actually can be quite variable and complex. Slight differences in sound can indicate major differences in attitudes and needs. If we recognize a dog's body language well enough to assist rather than compete against its attempts to fulfill survival needs, it will have less need to vocalize. Under the right conditions, it is definitely possible to have a quiet household.

Some people swear that their dogs try to talk to them in human language, but there are many skeptics. Actually, this notion may not be so far-fetched. Dogs do not have a person's vocal cords, and they cannot maneuver their facial muscles and tongues into forming as many different sounds, but many are adept at copying our behaviors, so some dogs may at least *try* to speak to us because of their adulation.

Birds probably do not plan what they are going to say, but several types of birds learn to speak many words and phrases with ease. This is mimicry at its finest, and submissive dogs also need to mimic their leaders. It would seem logical that some dogs might try to speak simple, necessary words like "out" and "food." They hear these words often and because of repetition, they respond correctly. Trying to say these words might be a logical extension of their instinctive need to go outside or to eat. Even if they do not speak, dogs might be thinking these words. Some dogs may silently mouth certain words on occasion. If you think your dog does this, watch to see if it repeats its behavior at the expected times. If so, this is another way you can understand your dog.

Even if some dogs try to speak human language, other forms of communication are much better developed. In addition to body language and barking, dogs make great use of eye contact and eye movements as well as urine, stool, anal sac, and body oil markings.

Eye contact is very important in dogs. When the more dominant dog stares down the other dog, many fights are avoided. In this situation, the dog that turns its eyes away first is proven more submissive, and it is not necessary then to try and determine dominance.

Ophthalmologists are unaware that any special energy emanates from an animal's eyes, but anyone who has found himself unable to keep his eyes focused on another person's stare must wonder. It is as if the more dominant person "burns" the eyes of the other person, and causes the eyes to water, the eyelids to flutter or close, and ultimately to turn away. The same thing happens with dogs; they can sometimes get our attention simply by staring at us When we turn our heads toward our dogs suddenly and find them looking at us, we may be reacting to the dog's stare.

Problems arise when two dogs are equally dominant (two submissive dogs might never look into each other's eyes). Fights to determine dominance are virtually guaranteed. The same situation can occur between a person and a dog. If both are equally dominant and try to stare down the other, the dog will likely fight the person. That is why we are told not to stare at a strange dog. We can avoid fights if we don't provide competition for dominant dogs.

Except for the most dominant and most submissive dogs, and certain unique breeds, we can distinguish the emotional states of many dogs by the appearance of their eyes, emotions such as happiness, fear, anger, sadness, confusion, frustration, and love. These changes are subtle and difficult to describe verbally, but with practice they can be recognized. We can practice on other people as well as on dogs, because there is little difference.

Dogs also use their eyes and heads to point a direction or to obtain something. A dog that wants to go outside may look at us until we respond, and then roll its eyes toward the door. More overtly, it may jerk its head toward the door as it rolls its eyes, as if it wants us to follow its head toward the object of its attention. It may be unnecessary for dogs that can get their point across with their eyes to jump up and down at the door (Fig. 13).

Dogs use urine, stool deposits, anal sac excretions, and body oils as territorial markers, to communicate with other animals. Dogs use these markers to communicate with us as well, especially when we misunderstand them.

These smell factors are so important that most dogs must sniff the ground within their territory daily to analyze and respond to the markings of other animals. These dogs need daily walks for this reason as much as for exercise. No matter how large their territory, they must urinate and defecate in strategic locations throughout its limits.

Dominant dogs place their urine and stool around the external boundaries of their circular territory. They lift their legs to urinate high up on objects such as trees, bushes, telephone

Fig. 13. This dog tells us it wants to go outside without barking or jumping.

poles, and fire hydrants which rise out of the ground. Dominant dogs are quick to urinate directly on top of the urine markings of territorial intruders. A dominant dog is not fulfilling its survival needs if it is not permitted to mark its territory to communicate its perception of itself.

Submissive dogs may urinate and defecate in one spot repeatedly, often in the center of their yard or territory and away from the markings of other animals. If they also have dominant tendencies, they may urinate on top of or next to the urine or stool deposits of other dogs. This behavior is not unlike that of a fisherman who leaves his baited hook in the water and returns periodically to check for a fish on the hook. Such dogs seem to return to the exact location of their previous markings to smell for animals that may have urinated or defecated there after them. This behavior does not always signify competition, because dogs seem to enjoy some of these smells enough to sniff contentedly for several minutes. Perhaps they are also advertising for mates.

Some highly submissive dogs have trouble utilizing their anal sacs except during severe fright, but others may spray a microscopic mist onto objects they wish to dominate. Anal sac material smells quite foul to many people, so it is difficult to imagine why dogs would wish to smell it. But it appears that each dog's anal sacs smell slightly different from all other dogs. It is like a calling card, to distinguish one from another besides serving as a territorial marker.

A dog's skin has a number of sebaceous glands that produce oil. This oil also has a unique smell and can be used to communicate. A dog that rubs its chin or cheeks on a person, door, or piece of furniture may be marking territory. Oil from the paws is rubbed onto the floor or ground with a backwards pushing action of the hind or front paws (Fig. 14). If you doubt these smells have any communicative value, take your dog on a walk through snow. Unless it is too fearful to explore the area, it may sniff specifically at the paw or footprints left in the snow by other animals and people. It may urinate or defecate on top of certain prints. Dogs smell these oil prints frequently throughout the year, but the snow helps us see what the dog can smell.

This discussion of territorial markers is important because dogs that are unable to fulfill survival needs in more subtle ways may urinate and defecate to compete with their owners. When our dogs eliminate wastes in the home, many of us become too frustrated to notice the location and timing of the deposit. But many "mistakes" in the home are purposeful forms of communication and result from competition with another animal or person.

If an indirectly dominant dog that is accustomed to laying on its owner's favorite chair is suddenly prevented from doing so, the next day, the owner may find a stool deposit and punish the dog. Afterwards, the dog repeats the behavior. This is a vicious cycle because the dog is used to dominating the chair

Fig. 14. This dog is marking territory by rubbing oils from his right front leg and left rear leg.

and/or the owner's lap, and when prevented from doing so in its usual way, it dominates the chair with a stool deposit. This is the dog's way of saying "my chair."

If this dog had been treated consistently, it wouldn't have had to mark the chair with stool. When it is punished (dominated) for marking the chair, the additional competition from the owner causes a second dominant reaction. If it is punished again, the next time it may chew on the chair. Letting the dog maintain its original dominance over the chair and the owner's lap would have prevented the stool marking behavior, and the dog would never have considered destructive chewing.

If a dog is accustomed to entering the bedroom, it may urinate or defecate on or next to the door if it is suddenly closed to

51

prevent the dog from entering. If the dog is used to sleeping on the bed, it may mark the bed when kicked off. If a dog is never permitted on the bed, it may pull the bedspread down onto the floor and lay on it (Fig. 15). It may then mark, chew or shred the bedspread if it is punished. If one family member competes against the dog, it may urinate or defecate on that person's clothes, bed, floor, etc. in specific response to the competition. In each case, the dog is talking to us as clearly as if it could speak our language.

Dogs have many methods of communicating with us, and we should not minimize their importance just because they exclude verbal language. At the same time, we should realize that dogs pick up on our body language, voice intonation, and other non-

Fig. 15. If a dog cannot dominate the owner's bed, it may dominate the bedspread.

verbal cues as communication with them. If we understand what a dog is communicating to us and how it perceives us, we can attain much understanding and positive interaction.

Chapter 5

HOW DOGS PERCEIVE US

It is important to understand a dog's general behavioral tendencies, but it is equally important to know how a dog perceives us. Many of a dog's daily activities come from interactions with its owners and other people. A dog's response to these interactions depends almost entirely on whether it perceives us as a friend or foe, leader or follower, helper or antagonist.

We cannot ask a dog what it thinks of us, but we can get an accurate assessment of its perception by looking at our own behavior and our dog's reactions to it. Unfortunately, many people have difficulty looking at themselves, especially when it might reveal human error or inconsistency. To refuse the opportunity for self-assessment is to guarantee conflicts between our dogs and ourselves.

Our biggest mistake is to pretend we are perfect and incapable of error since mistakes perpetuate themselves when we refuse to recognize them. Personal growth is possible only when we recognize our mistakes and consider alternatives which can help prevent them in the future. Observant people can experience personal growth by watching a dog's responses to their behavior. Many insights are possible by comparing our typical body language with a dog's body language as described in Table 1.

As dog owners, we should ask ourselves several questions: How do we respond to changes in our environment? Do we respond to these changes out of confidence, arrogance, or fear, rationally or emotionally? Who is the leader in the family unit? The husband, the wife, one of the children, everyone, no one, or the dog? Are we natural leaders or natural followers? How do dogs perceive our body language and voice intonation? Do we own dogs because we love them, or because they fulfill some of our own selfish needs? Can our dogs trust us to maximize their survival chances, or must they compete against us for survival?

We like to believe we are naturally superior to dogs. If this were completely true, all people would be good leaders for all dogs. However many dogs function as pack leaders in their own homes. Perhaps these dogs think they are naturally superior to people! If *we* are superior, we must prove it through our actions (body language) rather than our words and thoughts.

Dogs actually perceive little if any difference between themselves and people. It is a dog's natural tendency to live in a group or pack. Whether this group is composed of dogs, people, or a combination of the two, a dog needs to find and secure its place within the leadership ladder or pecking order. It makes little or no distinction between people and dogs. If a dog is a natural leader, it will try to gain leadership within the group whether the followers are dogs or people. If it is a follower, it will search for the group leader. If it has both dominant and submissive qualities, it will follow confident leader-type people, but will try to dominate fearful people.

Leadership Ladders

Before discussing the human-dog interaction, it is helpful to consider the leadership ladder of a hypothetical pack of twelve dogs. Dog number one is confident 90% of the time and is considered the pack leader by the other dogs, all of whom are less confident. This dog maintains its leadership position as long as it remains more confident than the other dogs. Dogs number two and three, with 80 percent and 70 percent confidence respectively, may occasionally challenge dog number one for leadership, especially during mating season.

Dog number one retains its lofty position until age, disease, or another stressful situation causes it to lose some of its confidence. At that point, dog number two will challenge it for supremacy. If the challenge is successful, the order changes, and dog number two takes the top spot. The loss of leadership may cause such a loss of confidence for the former leader that it may fall rapidly toward the bottom of the order. Because of its need to dominate, it may even lose the will to live if it cannot regain supremacy.

Dog number twelve is confident only 5 percent of the time. It may fear the most dominant dogs so much that it cannot even follow them. However, it can follow dogs number nine, ten, and eleven, and these dogs may be confident enough to follow dog number one. Each dog follows the dog above it in confidence, and the pack remains a functioning unit.

The largest number of dogs appear to fall in the middle range of confidence levels, and the same is true of people. In this hypothetical pack of twelve dogs, dogs number four, five, six, seven, and eight all have between 40 percent and 60 percent confidence. In the presence of strong leaders and weak followers, this middle group is content and willing to get along with each other. If we divide these five dogs into a separate pack, the close similarity in confidence levels induces competition to determine a new pack leader.

If dog number four has the most confidence, it will become the leader. However, even with 60 percent confidence, it will be too fearful to lead 40 percent of the time. If it is afraid of thunderstorms for example, its sudden loss of confidence may cause shifts in the leadership ladder. If during a thunderstorm dogs six, seven, five, and eight have more confidence, respectively, than dog number four, they may rise above dog number four by displaying dominant behaviors. In this case, dog number six takes over leadership.

This fluctuation may be temporary. When dog number four regains its confidence after the storm passes, it may rechallenge dog number six for leadership. In this group, many changes in the leadership ladder will occur as these dogs gain or lose confidence. There may be many conflicts over leadership because there is no true leader in the group.

This hypothetical situation is an example of what happens frequently between pets and people. That is why we must recognize our own tendencies and confidence levels. Whether we like it or not, dogs constantly examine our confidence levels to determine their place relative to us.

There is a difference between ego and confidence. A highly dominant person is actually egotistical and arrogant rather than confident. This arrogance may attract some dogs (submissive dogs may try to follow people indiscriminately), but it is not based on a firm foundation. Unlike confidence, arrogance crumbles into insecurity when a person is unable to dominate. Confidence levels are high only when these people are winners through dominance. Any loss destroys the confidence.

True confidence is present when we no longer need to prove ourselves. A dominant person continues to dominate in a constant attempt to prove himself superior. A submissive person continues to submit out of fear even when it is contraindicated, showing a complete lack of confidence. A truly confident person, and therefore the most attractive leader to a dog, is a person who knows when to dominate and when to submit, and can neither gain nor lose confidence by doing so.

A truly confident person has no fears and other negative emotions and is able to put aside personal worries and doubts long enough to consider the needs of the family dog. Dogs instantly recognize our fears. Confident dogs ignore fearful people, indirectly dominant dogs try to dominate them, and fearful dogs become even more fearful in their presence. Fear prevents some of us from serving the leadership role that pet dogs need from people.

All people have emotions, but we should not let them determine our behavior when dealing with our dogs. We must recognize that we are less capable of leadership until we can resolve our own problems. Our emotional changes induce behavior changes in our dogs that we should recognize. To ignore the important interrelationship between our own emotional states and our dog's behavior creates conflicts and problems for our dogs and ourselves.

Emotions can indicate a lack of confidence, and therefore a lack of leadership. When we feel personally dependent or inadequate, that indicates a follower role to dogs, and they will respond accordingly. If we admit by our manner that we need a dog for our survival more than it needs us, we are placing it in a position of leadership. It will then display dominant behaviors toward us to preserve its leadership. People ask veterinarians or psychologists to alter many of these behaviors for them. Such changes are impossible until we raise our own confidence levels. We must help ourselves in order to help our dogs.

It is not always good to feel sorry for a dog. Sick, injured, or weak dogs need our help. We are capable of providing valuable assistance but we can go too far. If our emotional attachment makes us excessively permissive, we do more harm than good. Permissiveness means submissiveness to dogs, and they may assume dominance over us despite their weak appearance. Even deformed runts need a good leader, and we cannot provide this leadership if we submit too often.

A middle-aged woman adopted a teacup poodle from an animal shelter because it had been abused by its previous owners and had inherited many physical problems. She believed she was helping the dog by saving it from unnecessary suffering, but her own emotional reaction gave the dog the opportunity to gain dominance over her.

The dog needed medication for heart disease, but it would bite anyone who tried to touch it or give it medication. It behaved the same way toward groomers, so its hair became matted and its skin got infected. The dog got large tufts of hair wrapped around its teeth because it bit at its infections. It desperately needed help but fought anyone who tried to get close.

This was an indirectly dominant dog with a great deal of fear. Its owner was so anxious to reverse the dog's early history of abuse that she refused to assume any kind of leadership role. She let this fairly submissive dog dominate her totally; it would even bite her on her hands every time it failed to get its way. The dog insisted on sleeping on the woman's left shoulder at night. Whenever she tried to move or roll over, the dog would bite her and force her to lay still.

The dog was totally in charge, but it was not a good leader. It was very nervous and it reacted out of fear rather than confidence. The owner's submissive attitude harmed the dog even though the woman thought she was helping. She permitted the dog to behave improperly so long that it was actually destroying itself. The dog died because it refused to accept the medication that could have reduced its suffering and prolonged its life.

The dog also suffered unnecessarily because of the woman's behavior. As a submissive follower, it needed a good leader to be emotionally content. The demands of leadership provided negative stress because it was not a natural leader.

People who think a dog misbehaves just to spite them show submissive selfishness and, therefore, a lack of leadership. A dog reacts to our behavior, and the results may annoy us. We should understand that the dog is just trying to stay in balance with its own nature. Most everything it does is designed to fulfill its own selfish needs. It probably does not consider its owner's feelings or selfishness, so it is not intentionally trying to hurt us. To think otherwise is to admit paranoia, inadequacy, and a lack of leadership confidence, and will encourage the dog to continue its behavior patterns to maintain its leadership position.

Job difficulties, money problems, marital spats, threatening weather conditions, cycles of failure, and other negative situations influence our attitudes and hence our confidence levels and leadership abilities. If we let these problems damage our own confidence levels, we influence the way our dogs perceive and respond to us. If our own dominant tendencies are inhibited too much during forced submission at work, we may exert excessive dominance at home to recreate our own natural balance. If we are more dominant than necessary, we may initiate a negative chain reaction and cause undue stress for our family and pets.

If we lose self-esteem because we must submit to employers too long, our own confidence levels may go down and we will be less capable of assuming a leadership role with our dogs. If they have any dominant tendencies, they may become the leaders; if they are highly fearful, our own loss of confidence may make them even more fearful.

We must try to develop and maintain our self-esteem despite personal problems so they do not also become problems for our pets and loved ones. We should not let losses reduce our confidence, or gains produce excessive arrogance so that we can help our dogs remain balanced as well.

Who is the leader in your home? Dogs look for the answer

to this question and we should, too. Conflicts between family members are a major cause of dog behavior problems. It is quite common for a husband and wife to disagree about how to handle their dog. Such conflict confuses a dog because it doesn't know who to follow. All family members should treat the dog the same way. If it must behave differently for each family member, it will behave unpredictably at best and destructively at worst.

It is helpful to examine the leadership ladder within the family structure to see how our dogs fit into this picture and how changes induce changes in dog behavior. As a hypothetical example, a middle-aged husband and wife have a balanced relationship with their pet dog. The husband is the family leader with 80 percent confidence, and both the wife, with 40 percent confidence, and the dog, with 60 percent confidence, accept his role. The husband's natural leadership qualities help all three get along well with each other. Although the dog has more confidence than the woman, it does not dominate the woman in her husband's presence.

The husband's death causes a drastic change in the leadership ladder if the wife cannot assume the leadership role. It causes both the wife and dog to lose confidence, because their dependent needs can no longer be satisfied, but since the dog now has the most confidence in the family, it takes over the leadership role. Because the dog is not highly confident, it will probably use indirect methods to dominate the woman.

Consider another situation where a husband and wife are both highly dominant, with 80 to 90 percent confidence levels, but own a submissive dog with only 40 percent confidence. Both people have a great deal of leadership confidence and their similarity induces competition over who is more dominant. As the two exchange leadership roles, their dog loses even more confidence because it is confused over whom to follow. It begins to exhibit submissive behavior problems as its confidence level dips to 20 percent or lower. The husband and wife must stop competing; they should share leadership in order to improve their dog's confidence and its behavior.

In many family situations, changes in the leadership ladder can occur frequently, especially when people and their dogs have similar confidence levels that can rise or fall quickly. For example, a husband, wife and dog all have between 40 and 60 percent confidence during normal conditions. When the husband loses his job, he also loses a great deal of confidence. The family may be forced to move to a smaller, less expensive home, and the wife gains some confidence from the opportunity to set up a new home and to provide moral support for her husband. At first the dog loses a little confidence because of the sudden change in home territory and because its former leader went from 60 to 20 percent confidence. Since the dog is capable of as much leadership as the wife, it could respond in one of two ways. If the dog is confident enough to demonstrate dominant instincts, it could begin to compete with the wife for leadership. If it competes successfully, it will be the new leader in the home. Or, if the dog loses confidence, it could begin to compete with the husband for second place in the home. Whoever loses the competition will be lowest on the leadership ladder and may lose even more confidence.

The Threat of Human Competition

If we are consistently more confident and therefore better leaders than our dogs, they will follow us. If we are less confident, they will lead us. If confidence levels are similar, there will be competition. This forces behavior changes in dogs and causes many problems.

A seven-year-old uncastrated male Lhasa Apso named Sammie was allowed to dominate his owner after her husband died. She openly admitted that she needed his companionship, and she doubted the dog could need her as much as she needed it. As a result, she accepted many of Sammie's dominant behaviors. She let him jump up on her whenever he wanted, bite at her ankles whenever she walked away from him, urinate in the house, and steal food from the table. She permitted Sammie to mount her arms and legs and ejaculate sperm.

The woman was afraid to assert herself because she felt dependent and inadequate: She didn't want to hurt Sammie's feelings, so she tolerated behaviors she really didn't like. Unfortunately, she didn't realize that Sammie was not naturally dominant (except perhaps during mating season) and her permissiveness hurt more than it helped. She also did not realize that by permitting Sammie to be dominant, she encouraged even more behavior change.

Eventually, Sammie demanded the opportunity to dominate both indirectly and directly more frequently than ever before. He began to chew up the furniture whenever his owner was away at work, as if to seek revenge for her leaving his territory. He wanted to go outside more frequently, to expand the boundaries of his territory. He actually destroyed a large wooden door while scratching to get outside.

Sammie showed certain dominant tendencies, but he was actually a mixture of dominant and submissive and would have accepted leadership from many people. But when he was in charge, there were many problems. Finally, when the woman became emotionally upset over the increased destructiveness, although Sammie was well-behaved in her presence, she began to compete with him for leadership.

The woman did not understand how to be a good leader, and she did not understand her dog. Without realizing it, she allowed her emotions to dictate her response to situations. As Sammie became more destructive, she got more upset and therefore more insecure. Since she could no longer trust Sammie, she locked him in the bedroom when she was away at work. Though the owner thought isolation would solve her problem, it made Sammie's problems worse. His actions were trying to tell her that he was dominant and wanted more territory, but he also demanded to be the center of her attention at all times. This seeming contradiction is common in mixed-behavior dogs who try to be both dominant and submissive at the same time. This shows that they are not really leaders and that they need human understanding and leadership.

Isolation was the exact opposite of what Sammie needed. It was a competitive threat to his leadership position. The woman decided to fight with him, which induced additional competitive reactions, when she should have risen above him through understanding. A chain reaction was inevitable.

As a dominant response to a not-so-dominant competitor, Sammie shredded the bedroom door with his nails and chewed a bedspread and the woman's clothes. He wanted more territory, not less, so he tried to dig his way free from the isolation. He wanted to dominate his owner; in her absence, he dominated her bed and clothes.

The woman responded to Sammie's destructive behavior by tying him to the kitchen table with a leash that was too short to reach any furniture except the metal table. The woman thought Sammie could no longer destroy anything when she was away, but when she returned home the first day Sammie was tied in the kitchen, she discovered that the living room rug and half the furniture had been moved into the kitchen. She thought vandals were responsible, but nothing had been broken or stolen. Little seven-pound Sammie had grabbed the rug in his mouth and dragged it and the furniture on top of it into the kitchen. His reaction was so strong, he was able to move objects too heavy for him under normal circumstances. The more the woman competed against him, the stronger he became in order to win the battle. The owner didn't consider Sammie's feelings or his own competitive response to her attempts at dominance. In dog language he was telling her, "As a leader, I need more territory, not less. If you won't let me go after more territory, I'll bring it to me." He couldn't go into the living room, so he brought it to him.

Sadly, Sammie won the battle but lost the war. His owner became convinced she could not and should not become Sammie's leader, and she stopped competing with him. She decided she could never trust him at home alone, even though Sammie had no behavior problems while her husband was alive. She let Sammie have the run of the house because she felt helpless, and he virtually destroyed it.

Because Sammie was not a leader, assuming a leadership role made him a nervous wreck. In order to stay healthy, he needed to be a follower. The stresses of leadership contributed to health problems such as skin diseases from self-mutilation, prostate enlargement, a bladder infection, and ultimately, heart problems. In the end, Sammie was painlessly put to death.

Isolation is a severe example of how we compete with our dogs, but there are many other ways as well. If a dog thinks we are competing with it, it presumes we are doing so because we are similar. The dog instinctively responds in kind. It doesn't matter whether *we* think we are competing with our dogs, it is what *they* think that counts. If we compete, they will compete until there is a winner and a loser.

We compete with a dog whenever we go against its natural instincts. Sammie needed more territory and was forced to accept even less than normal. His destructiveness was predictable under these circumstances, but he was being punished for being himself. He would have been better off if he had found out on his own the limitations of his leadership abilities. If he had been given more territory than he could dominate effectively, he might have lost confidence and preferred staying inside thereafter.

Many pet dogs are punished for their normal behaviors, and this can be harmful. If a dog reacts only out of instinct, how can we blame it for behaving differently than we might in the same circumstance? Hunting dogs need to hunt, so we compete against them if we prevent them from enjoying hunting opportunities or punish them for doing so. Lap dogs need occasional opportunities to jump up on our laps, so knocking them off our laps competes against them. It is competition to lock up dogs with strong running instincts in areas too small to provide running opportunities. All dogs need to follow sexual drives during mating season, and punishing sexual behavior is a common form of competition for many dogs.

Human beings have instincts, too. We sometimes react before we think. These reactions either cause or result from competitive threats to our own welfare. People who have trouble waking up in the morning may be annoyed by a dog who is barking for food. Without thinking, we may yell at the dog or lash out, arms flailing. If we were less impulsive, we would realize that we are fighting with the dog over who can be more selfish: the dog wants its food and we want to sleep longer. Such forms of competition are common because we don't always think before we act.

Different dogs respond differently to our competition. Highly dominant dogs may actually enjoy competition as an opportunity to prove superiority. Like the king of the hill game, the one who makes it to the top becomes bored with success after a while if no one else tries to compete for the top position. Most of the satisfaction comes from the competition. On the other hand, highly submissive dogs are afraid of competition and often lose confidence at the mere suggestion of competition. Since they tend to take things personally, any raised voice or subtle attempt to dominate them can induce fear. Such a dog may assume we are a threat any time we react emotionally to a personal problem, even if it does not pertain to the dog.

Overcrowding is a major competitive problem for dogs. Submissive animals require much less space than dominant ones, but even submissive dogs can feel a threat to their territorial integrity if they are forced to live in a home that is too small or that houses too many other people or animals.

The dog's size is less important than its psychological needs for territory in determining whether it can live comfortably in a home with one person or more. One thing is certain: if a dog acts like it needs more territory than it already has, it should not be moved to smaller quarters or be forced to live with additional animals or people. A dog who is trying to establish and maintain its own territory could perceive that as competition. Even if it behaves well during the summer, the negative effects of cabin fever during cold winter months can produce behavior problems as more family members are locked inside the home for longer periods.

Even a person who is usually a good leader for dogs can have bad days. When this happens, a sudden loss of confidence may place this person closer to his or her dog on the leadership ladder. The dog may then sense an opportunity to compete for leadership. Such changes are usually subtle and transitory as long as the person regains confidence. If the pattern of the bad day is prolonged, continuous competition may well result.

Whether we like the idea or not, some dogs perceive themselves as being better (or at least no worse) than humans. When they feel this way, they are not going to understand why they cannot have the things we have or do the things we do. A dog might expect to be able to enter every room we enter, eat what we eat, and do what we do. If we must restrict the dog's activity, we must first act like a good leader and try to help it rather than compete against it. To compete is to demonstrate our lack of superiority and our lack of leadership ability. To fulfill our role properly, we must rise above the competition. We must ignore our own selfish needs, injuries, and pressures and observe instead the reality of our dog's behavior. If we are better than dogs, we must prove it with actions rather than inflated egos.

Chapter 6

DEVELOPING MUTUAL TRUST

In Sammie's case, described in the previous chapter, the owner could not trust Sammie and Sammie could not trust his owner. This arose from negative competition and put a severe barrier between the person and the dog. This barrier prevented any kind of compatible relationship.

There is a strong bond which brings dogs and people together. This loving attraction has existed ever since dogs and people first started helping each other. It is the main reason we get along as well as we do. For most people, this attractive force is stronger than our need to compete against dogs, but it is less recognizable when trust is lost. Sammie and his owner had a good relationship at the beginning, but they learned to distrust each other and the relationship deteriorated.

Love between dogs and people appears instinctive. Trust is a natural result of this love, so unless we do something to prevent it, trust is guaranteed. Because pet dogs love people, they tend to have a positive first impression of most people. They approach and befriend us because they trust us. When we let them down by competing against them or by behaving inconsistently, we inhibit the attracting forces by reducing trust.

Some people think that once a dog misbehaves, it can never be trusted again. This is totally false. Dogs are creatures of habit, just like we are, and once certain behaviors are reinforced they are quick to use them again and again. But if a mutual bond of love between dog and person ever existed, it can be again. If something can be done to improve mutual trust, a dog's behavior will improve, as it enjoys the fruits of love. If the love can be rekindled, trust, and therefore behavior, will improve accordingly.

The human-dog bond is stronger in some instances than in others. Many problems that dogs cause are inevitable; they come from incompatibility between dogs and people. Dogs can't change totally, and neither can we. The best way to insure compatibility and fewer behavior problems is to select a puppy that will fit best into the family, and then to carefully establish a relationship that can stand the test of time.

Unfortunately, some people select dogs because of appearance, utility, or their own emotional reactions, rather than through a careful analysis of behavioral compatibility. As a result, a submissive person may select the most dominant puppy in a litter, and a dominant person may select a weak, fearful dog. Neither situation is suitable for the puppy or the person, and problems are inevitable.

It is important to examine a puppy's general behavior tendencies and the strength of its attraction to its potential owners. No two puppies will behave exactly the same way toward us, so we should test a number of puppies to see which ones behave the best in our presence and have the strongest loving attraction to us. This may be time consuming, but it is worthwhile to try and prevent behavioral incompatibility.

Many behaviorists recommend a series of tests for selecting a puppy. They are designed to determine a puppy's degree of natural attraction to prospective owners. A puppy that ignores or walks away from us is too independent and has too little attraction to make a good pet for us. A puppy that reacts aggressively toward dominant handling may never accept a subordinant position and is a high risk pet for elderly people or families with children (Fig. 16). Conversely, a pup that cowers with head lowered and tail between its legs is probably too fearful of our dominance and is incompatible with us. A pup that bites at our ankles as we walk away from it is not doing it out of love (Fig. 17). The most ideal puppy is the one that has a natural attraction to us, a willingness to follow us happily and to submit to our dominance without fear (Fig. 18).

Most veterinarians advise their clients to buy or adopt puppies from retailers, breeders, or shelters that strive to insure quality control. Health problems adversely affect a dog's behavior; pups sold by people who do not follow routine health and sanitation guidelines are poor risks. Severe environmental stress during the first few weeks of a pup's life can stimulate

Fig. 16. A puppy suitable for you will permit you to pick it up.

and reinforce behavioral reactions that are too extreme for most new pet owners to modify. Excessive isolation or rough handling can have a negative effect on an impressionable puppy's perspective of life. Behavior problems are frequently hereditary. The best bet is to obtain a pup from people who offer guarantees and provide complete health and behavioral histories of the puppy's ancestors.

Hopefully, retailers, breeders, and others involved in the dog exchange business care enough about the welfare of their dogs to refuse to place a dog with poor-risk owners. There are some puppies that may prove to be unsuitable as pets, and there are as many people who are unsuitable as dog owners. Discussions between seller and buyer can help determine which people and which dogs are best suited to one another.

Fig. 17. A puppy that bites at your ankles is a poor-risk pet for you.

Fig. 18. The right dog for you has a strong loving attraction for you.

Dogs can suffer unnecessary, severe problems if they are forced to live with unsuitable owners. This is an extreme example: A young woman purchased a dachshund puppy from a large, reputable pet store that offered a generous guarantee. Any dog with health problems could be exchanged within seven days of purchase. Four or five days after she bought her dog, the woman returned the puppy, dead and with bruises all over its body. No autopsy was performed, and she selected another puppy as part of her guarantee. She said she had no idea what caused the first pup's death.

The woman returned the second puppy, also dead. She claimed it may have been run over by a car. There was no evidence of bone fractures typical of automobile accidents, but again no autopsy was performed. She took home a third and fourth dachshund puppy and returned each one dead.

Her confusing explanation that the fourth puppy may have been trapped behind a washing machine prompted an autopsy. The dog's liver, spleen, and lungs had been severed into many small pieces, consistent with extreme physical abuse. The woman was probably so dominant that she squeezed the puppy's fragile body too hard and killed it. Such a person should never be in close contact with a dog.

The mutual trust created by a sound selection process should be reinforced as soon as a puppy arrives at its new home. We must socialize a pup properly and teach it family rules. House-training, establishing regular diet and feeding schedules, and determining where the dog will sleep are all part of the early relationship. The techniques used to establish acceptable routines are important and provide opportunities to also establish mutual trust.

There are different theories about the merits of reward versus punishment in dog training. There are times when minimal forms of punishment are required, but reward for positive behaviors is the most consistent means of encouraging behavioral repetition. Some dogs will do almost anything for food snacks, so many people train dogs by giving food treats in exchange for proper behavior. Too many snacks increases the likelihood of obesity and its physical complications, however, and it inhibits housetraining by stimulating waste elimination reflexes too frequently. There is a better reward than food.

Praise and petting on the chest and neck is the best reward for proper behavior. Dogs need love more than anything else, so they tend to repeat behaviors we reinforce with love in order to receive more. Dogs need confidence-builders to counterbalance their submissive role toward their leaders. We should praise a puppy whenever it listens to our orders. A pup should also be praised for spontaneous positive behaviors, when it lays down and relaxes, doesn't beg at the table, acts content during fear-inducing situations such as thunderstorms, fireworks, territorial intruders, and sudden noises, and asks to go outside for waste elimination. Praise and love can only have positive ramifications, unless they are used to reinforce negative behaviors.

We should resort to physical punishment only when absolutely necessary. It should be used to get the dog's attention rather than to proclaim extreme dominance. Dogs remember their previous behaviors for no more than a few seconds, so any punishment after this time doesn't connect with the behavior and can only harm the dog. Spanking serves a useful purpose only when the dog is caught in the act. If your dog nips at you, give it one quick slap to the muzzle to remind it that you are more dominant. Use subtle dominant methods so that more severe competitve fights are not necessary. We don't want to hurt dogs, even if we think they have hurt us. We do not want to make them obey us out of fear, either. We simply wish to remind them which behavior is acceptable.

Perhaps the most useful punishment technique is to look a dog right in the eye and say, "No!" in a stern, firm voice. If we really mean it, and lower our voice for a more dominant tone quality, most dogs will stop their negative behaviors on the spot. Yelling and screaming is not effective, and can make a dog unnecessarily fearful. But a firm "No!" followed by praise and petting upon compliance, sets behavioral limits without need for physical domination.

Although praise and petting serve important functions, it's not a good idea to use them too often. If we pet too often for no reason other than to fulfill our own dependent needs for love and physical contact, a dog can become overly dependent or spoiled. If it enjoys being touched so much that it falls down in ecstasy every time it is petted, a dog may seek this contact all the time and may become angry or frustrated over a lack of attention. Since subordinate dogs rub, groom, and provide physical contact to pack leaders, a dog that is petted too much can mistakenly think it is the leader.

There is no single guaranteed method for training dogs. Since a dog may behave differently toward different people, each of us should seek to find, and stick to, the combination of actions and attitudes that works best for our dog. It is very important for every family member to agree on training methods and to share in the responsibilities of leadership. This adds to the consistency and stability of the environment and gives the dog more opportunities to practice the behaviors the family wishes it to use. Dogs whose families are divided over whether to train by punishment or reward, and what individual roles should be, have many behavior problems. Without agreement, success is unlikely.

Perhaps the best way to develop and maintain mutual trust is to understand a dog well enough to help it balance its opposite dominant and submissive survival needs on a daily basis. This requires a willingness to compromise at times, but any temporary sacrifice can be well worth the effort.

Since we know that a dog *must* use certain dominant and submissive behaviors, we should permit those which are tolerable and occur most frequently. We know that the dog will use more overt and potentially negative behaviors if subtle ones fail to fulfill survival needs, so we must also be prepared to prevent extremes.

We must be willing to set limits when necessary. If the dog is taking over too much leadership in the home, we should assert our own dominance. If the dog is becoming too fearful, we should soften our voices, lower our body posture so it can be perceived as less dominant, and reassure the dog that nothing can harm it. If the dog is indirectly dominant and spoiled, we should place some limits on its selfishness. We should help lower the dog's confidence level if it is too dominant, and raise its confidence if it is too submissive.

An excellent way to establish leadership and to help a dog balance instinctive needs is simple command-response training. Walk your dog on leash at least once a day. Place the dog on your left side and help it to walk at your side. If the dog pulls ahead of you, give the leash a sharp, quick tug to draw it back. If the dog is stubborn or fearful and lags behind you, reassure it and coax it forward, but don't pull it. Every time the dog complies with your wishes, praise it and pet it on the chest and neck.

When you stand to the right of the dog, you have the leadership position. If you place your left hand on the dog's shoulders, you dominate it and push its spirits downward. The dog's confidence improves when you pet its chest and neck with your palm up, a submissive jesture. Command-response training gives us the opportunity to prove true leadership by alternately dominating and submitting to the dog through body language and voice intonation.

As you walk your dog, give it a few simple commands to learn. With a low, firm voice, tell it to "Stop," "Stay," "Sit," "Heel." The voice intonation should indicate that you are giving the dog an order. At first, you may have to use your hands in a dominant fashion to place the dog's body in the position you require. When the dog responds properly, pet it on the chest and neck and use a higher-pitched voice to praise it. This not only balances out your dominance, but encourages the dog to repeat the behavior. The dog will learn quickly. Two ten-minute command-response exercises on a daily basis will establish and maintain your leadership (Figs. 19 and 20).

The way you hold the leash also influences the way your dog perceives you. If you jerk the leash at appropriate times, that can serve a useful purpose. Once the dog understands its role though, it should be free to walk at your side without undue leash tension. If you hold the leash too tightly, your extra dominance indicates to the dog that you do not trust it to behave properly. And if the dog desires a degree of independence, letting the leash hang loose helps it to maintain a feeling of freedom as it complies with your wishes.

Command-response training should also be practiced without

Fig. 19. Everyone should develop as good a relationship with their dog as this man. Mutual trust and respect guarantee a positive relationship.

Fig. 20. With command-response training, a dog will sit immediately on command.

a leash. Leash restraint helps facilitate early training, and it protects dogs from motor vehicles and other dangers. But constant leash restraint can serve as a too-dominant factor working against a dog's self-confidence. If a dog obeys your orders on leash, it should also obey off the leash. Eliminating the leash can improve the trusting relationship between you and your dog. It gives you the satisfaction of knowing the dog is obeying even though it could run away if it so desired.

We don't have to be expert animal trainers to fill a leadership role with dogs. We simply need to know when to be dominant and when to be submissive, and to have the self-confidence to feel comfortable in a leadership position. We can learn the mechanics of command-response training by taking our dogs to obedience training classes run by people who are successful leaders for dogs. These people can train most of the pets they encounter. Dogs often forget their training though, if it is not continued at home, no matter how well they performed for their trainers. First, the people best equipped to be perceived as leaders by dogs often become animal trainers. Most dogs respond better for them than for their owners. Second, many of us are either unwilling or unable to consistently act like leaders at home.

Ideally, entire families should take their dogs to obedience training class if this training is wanted or needed. Everyone in the family should take turns practicing command-response training with the dog so it learns how to obey commands while each family member learns how to function as a leader. The dog can develop a feeling of mutual trust with each family member and reduce the likelihood of competition at home. Command-response training is much less valuable if it is not used consistently by all family members.

Self-confidence is a more difficult problem for many people. All the knowledge in the world cannot help us be leaders for dogs if we lack self-confidence. We cannot hide our fears and self–doubts from our dogs, so we should try to improve ourselves. Everyone has the potential to function as a leader for at least some dogs, and we should all possess the confidence to know this.

It is quite common to doubt our own abilities, but that doesn't mean our doubts are valid. Many people mistrust their dogs just because they do not think their orders can be taken seriously. This is unfair to the dog that sees our leadership potential and looks for us to provide it. If a dog thinks we can act like a leader, then maybe we can. We may need to practice our technique and to learn from our mistakes in order to raise our confidence levels. When we are more confident, we are better leaders. If we don't let the daily irritations of life get us down, we will have more survival confidence than our dogs and we will be better prepared for leadership.

As a test of your leadership and trust, try the following: Give your dog the order to "Stay," and then walk away confidently without looking back to check the dog's compliance. If you need to turn around to see if the dog has moved, you do not trust your dog enough. If the dog has disobeyed by the time you turn around, it does not respect you enough. In the ideal relationship, the dog obeys you completely and you praise it for doing so. Adjustments are necessary if either you or the dog failed to complete the test satisfactorily.

We often procrastinate and forget about our leadership responsibilities. Leadership *is* sometimes difficult when we have our own dependent needs. Nevertheless, we should use command-response training every day even if the dog's behavior is causing no problems. We may not always have to behave like responsible leaders, but there are times when we have no choice and must control a dog's behavioral tendencies. If we have developed a trusting relationship and have practiced our responsibilities all along, we can trust our dogs to obey us when the situation requires it.

We also need to know how to handle behavior change so that it will not deteriorate over time. If we notice our dog is trying to get its way too much but we fail to do anything about it, we have reinforced the behavior by not inhibiting it. This will encourage the dog to continue similar behavior tendencies, and it will provide the repetition necessary to change a one-time behavior into a perpetual habit.

When you doubt how best to interact with your dog, ask

yourself how you would want to be treated under similar circumstances. If you act like you trust your dog, it will behave in a trustworthy manner and will trust you as well.

It is extremely important that a leader's behavior be consistent. Dogs like a daily routine, so we should help by establishing and maintaining regular schedules. We should consider our dog's needs as well as our own, and we should not lie to our dogs by changing our own rules too often. If we permit a behavior one time but not the next, we confuse a dog and reduce trust. We should establish fair rules and stick to them. Our dogs need this consistency from their human leaders.

Before we react to behaviors we dislike, we should examine the situation carefully. If the dog is behaving badly without just cause, we should work with it to correct its behavior. If we are the cause of the behavior change, we should be courageous enough to admit our errors to ourselves and our dog. We should apologize directly to our dog and try to learn how to correct our mistake. If the dog is not at fault, we should not blame it. Trust requires accurate understanding.

We all have a few squabbles with our dogs, but we should not let these temporary disagreements spoil the opportunity for a long-term relationship. We should make up with our dogs after every conflict. We may have been upset for the moment, but our disagreement arose from one particular set of circumstances. Since we still love our dogs, we should not let a few squabbles inhibit these positive feelings. Our dogs will trust us more if we remember to show them our love.

Chapter 7

THE VALUE OF OPPOSITES

Dominant and submissive instincts are opposites which work together best when they are balanced. This knowledge can simplify our understanding of dog behavior and our ability to prevent and correct behavioral extremes. We do not have to memorize numerous recommendations for behavior modification. If we understand the importance of opposites, we can devise our own behavior modification techniques by finding the cause of the problem and reversing the process.

There appears to be a straight-line back-and-forth relationship between confidence levels and behavior. As a dog increases its self-confidence it becomes more dominant, and as it loses confidence, it becomes more submissive. If we can modify a dog's confidence level, we can modify its behavior.

An extremely submissive dog that has problems such as fear-biting or submissive wetting needs more confidence to behave better, so we must provide security, love, and reassurance. An extremely dominant dog that bites aggressively or housesoils for territorial supremacy needs a firm leader to reduce its arrogance enough so it will submit to the leader.

Our own confidence levels influence whether dogs perceive us as dominant or submissive. Since dogs adjust their own confidence levels to either dominate or submit to us (to find their place on the leadership ladder), we can also modify a dog's behavior by adjusting our own confidence levels (see Chapter 8).

If our dominance scares dogs with submissive behavior problems, we must be less arrogant; they need us to be more confident if our own insecurities and fears demonstrate our lack of leadership. Conversely, dogs with dominant behavior problems need us to be more confident if our lack of leadership causes them to assume leadership; they need us to be less arrogant if our own dominant needs create a competitive conflict. Dogs are likely to demonstrate balanced behavior if we remain consistent, stable, and balanced, and display a relaxed confidence which requires neither dominance nor submission.

Controlling Extremes

We can use our knowledge of opposites to control simple and complex behavior problems. A dog that is extremely fearful may panic and do the exact opposite of what it needs to do in order to help itself. If a fearful dog is placed in a cage in an unfamiliar environment, it may become extremely nervous because of the strange sights, sounds, and smells. If panic sets in, the dog may die of heat stroke. This dog could remain healthy if it relaxed without fear, but panic almost always causes self-destructive behavior. We can best prevent self-destructive panic by reducing a dog's fears and increasing its confidence level.

An extremely dominant dog will almost always do the exact opposite of what it is ordered to do, so we can utilize reverse psychology to control its behavior. If we order the dog to do the exact opposite of what we wish it to do, it will likely behave the opposite of our order and do what we wish. If we want a dominant dog to come to us, we should ignore it, since ordering it to come to us may cause it to walk away. Or, we should order it to stay away from us. If we want the dog to stop its status howling at night, we can induce compliance more quickly by saying "Good dog" than by yelling obscenities at it.

If one approach makes a dog's behavior worse, we should use an opposite approach to try and improve the behavior. If we cause a problem by insisting that the dog always behave as we wish, we should let the dog occasionally do what it wishes. If the dog gets its way too often and causes a problem, we should help it fulfill its needs when we want it to.

The best way to stop a dog from using certain negative behaviors as attention-getters is to ignore it. If a dog cowers or engages in submissive wetting when we speak loudly to it, we should soften our voices. If a dog wets submissively when we approach it to love it, we should walk away. We should lay down on our backs and praise the dog only when it is confident enough to walk over to us. If isolation increases a dog's frustration reactions, it should be given more territory than it could possibly dominate, rather than less. In addition, it should be given intense physical exercise on a daily basis to satisfy all its dominant needs and thus permit it to accept confinement more readily. If a dog reacts fearfully to unusual or inconsistent noises or to visitors, we should expose it to these stimuli so often that it no longer reacts to them.

Many dog behavior problems are induced by changes in our own attitudes and confidence levels. In these cases, we should evaluate our own behavior honestly so that we can make the modifications necessary to reverse the behavior. Simple problems often become complex because we overreact. At the first sign of a problem, people begin to worry and to respond to their dogs on a more emotional level. Generally, our losses of confidence make the behavior worse rather than better. The best approach is to relax and stop worrying in order to prevent a negative chain reaction. If the dog usually behaves well, we should not assume there is a major problem just because the dog makes an occasional mistake. Perhaps the dog is just having a bad day and will not repeat the behavior tomorrow. If we can balance our own emotional and behavioral extremes, we will help balance our dog's behavior as well.

Problems may arise even in homes with the most suitable environment for a dog. When this happens we can prevent complex problems by resolving the simple ones. Even in the most complex situations, many, if not all, problems can be eliminated if we use our knowledge of opposites to reverse the process. If you doubt this approach, consider these four cases. In each instance, behavior problems were corrected by determining the cause of the problem and utilizing an opposite approach to change the behavior.

● The owners of a three-year-old female golden retriever built an outdoor fenced pen with a gravel base for the dog to use for eliminating waste. The owners forced the dog to go to it six times a day, whether it needed to or not, to teach it how to use the pen.

At first, the dog went to the pen readily, but it became more and more reluctant to go out as time went on. It would roll over onto its back at pen time, an act its owners considered cute. Eventually, the owners had to literally drag the dog to the pen. Since the dog loved to go out the front door because its owners would take it for walks and on trips, the owners were baffled about why the dog was so reluctant to go out the back door.

The owners were actually forcing submission in excess of the dog's actual needs. This is obvious from the dog's increasingly submissive behavior. The problem was resolved simply by having the dog go to the pen when it needed to rather than when the owners forced it to. The dog only needed to use the pen two or three times a day, and it was much more willing to go out to the pen when it could make its own decisions. As soon as the initial procedure was reversed, the dog's behavior improved.

● A four-year-old female German shepherd chewed the furniture while its owners were away. It would scratch at the front window whenever it saw the mailman, meter reader, or other neighborhood animals walk onto its territory. The owners decided to isolate the dog in their family room when they were gone, to prevent the window scratching, but isolation made the chewing worse.

There were two main causes of the behavior problems. The dog was strongly attracted to the man of the house, but he was irritated by his leadership responsibilities and he pushed the dog away, out of competition, whenever she approached him. He didn't trust her to behave well in his absence and assumed a negative attitude toward her. The window in question provided an open view of all territorial intruders, and the dog was too protective of its outdoor territory to accept these intruders without an aggressive response.

By putting an outdoor shade on the window, that problem was solved. When the dog could not see the territorial intruders, it no longer reacted by scratching the window. When both owners reversed their attitudes, pretended a relaxed confidence, and decided to trust the dog more, the dog stopped its destructive chewing. The man stopped competing against the dog while he was home by accepting his responsibility to provide attention, love, and secure leadership. In fact, the dog stopped seeking as much attention because the man reversed his attitude and acted like he wanted the dog by his side all the time. The owners also stopped isolating the dog and reduced its frustration by giving it more territory rather than less. Both the window and chewing problems stopped quickly.

• A six-year-old male cockapoo was a good dog; its behavior conformed readily to the needs of its owners, with one exception. When it was alone and confronted by a sudden thunderstorm, it would panic. The dog would dig holes in the couch and rugs, as if trying to escape the unpredictable, fear-inducing thunder by creating a subterranean hiding place.

If the owners had punished the dog for its digging, they would have created a negative chain reaction by treating the result rather than the cause. Since thunderstorms do not occur frequently enough for some dogs to become accustomed to them, the owners played a recording of thunderstorms over and over. The dog finally learned to tune out the noise because of familiarity. The digging stopped completely, an example of how the opposite approach is successful in dealing with a dog's negative behavior.

• A two-year-old female German shepherd had some frightening experiences in the two homes she lived in as a puppy. She was a submissive dog, and her bad experiences had caused her to overreact to people with dominant tendencies. Through a combination of fear and negative reinforcement, the dog had developed a problem with uncontrollable submissive wetting.

The third owners loved the dog and wanted to save it from excessive abuse, so they adopted it. They understood that the dog was not wetting in the house on purpose, but the behavior still irritated them. If the man of the house raised his voice even slightly, the dog would dribble urine and then lick it up. The dog had a complete physical examination by several different veterinarians who determined that there was no physical defect, but the owners were still frustrated by the housesoiling.

These tensions reached a climax when the husband returned

home one day and found some diarrheic stool on the floor. He was furious, and he punished the dog severely for her mistake. The dog was usually submissive enough to stay close to home even when escape opportunities were present, but the severe punishment made it run away from home.

Two weeks later, emaciated and near death, the dog limped reluctantly back home. The owners were so grateful to have their dog back that they reversed their attitude and began to provide the softness, love, and extra attention necessary to increase the dog's confidence level. The man apologized to the dog for his misunderstanding and began to develop a stronger relationship with it. In addition, the owners began to ignore the submissive wetting so they wouldn't encourage the dog to use the behavior to get their attention.

Since the wetting problem had become habitual, it was not going to stop completely on the first day of the owners' attitude reversal. In the next three weeks, the dog had only two accidents, instead of two or three daily episodes. In time, the submissive wetting occurred only during extremely unusual fear-inducing situations. It was attitude reversal that helped improve the dog's behavior.

If we understand the value of opposites, we need only learn the specific cause of a behavior problem. If we can reverse the cause, we can also reverse the behavior. In the absence of physical or mental defects, there are often simple solutions for many seemingly complex behavior problems.

Chapter 8

TREATING PROBLEMS THROUGH ATTITUDE ADJUSTMENT

A toy poodle had undergone surgery for weak knee caps. The legs were completely healed within two weeks of surgery, but the dog continued to limp two months later. The owner felt sorry for it and continued to pamper and spoil it.

When a friend noticed that the dog limped only in front of the owner and showed no pain when left alone, the owner exclaimed, "Well that little dickens! She is just a spoiled brat. I sure know how to handle the situation now!"

That is an attitude adjustment.

Sometimes, we become so involved with our dogs that we fail to see the overall picture. We don't stop participating in the interaction long enough to observe the actual situation. We let our emotions prevent us from understanding the reasons behind our dogs' behavior and how we contribute to behavior problems. Our attitudes are a major cause of dog behavior problems.

A long-term relationship can be a positive learning experience for dogs and their owners, but only if we recognize and accept responsibility for our own errors. We can learn more from our failures than from our successes, but we cannot learn to improve the relationship as long as we pretend we are always perfect and our dogs are always wrong.

If we put our emotions aside and rise above the conflict, the insight gained from our observations is usually strong enough to improve our attitudes and behaviors toward our dogs. The truth of the situation becomes so obvious that correction procedures become equally obvious. The woman described above knew immediately that she must stop spoiling her dog once the sympathy lameness became obvious.

The following case clearly shows the difference between an owner's initial perception of his dog's behavior problems and the actual situation, and how the man's attitude adjustment led to improvement in his dog's behavior.

Sandy was a one-year-old female cockapoo who was owned by an unmarried, male doctor. The owner's major complaint was Sandy's destructive chewing of furniture. She was also too aggressive toward people. She jumped up on them, instigated fights, and bit at their ankles when they walked away from her. Sandy barked and howled excessively; she demonstrated digging and scratching behaviors which were destructive; she stole food from the kitchen table.

The doctor considered Sandy too dominant because of the destructiveness and the way she pulled on the leash during walks. But Sandy sometimes housesoiled when she was frightened by sudden noises and she licked her front legs raw, both submissive behaviors.

The owner had taught Sandy general commands like "Sit," "Stay," and "Fetch," but vocal correction was no longer effective. When she was punished with a rolled newspaper, she went off to a corner to lick herself, and the chewing continued whenever the owner was away. He even tried a muzzle, but Sandy would work at it until she got it off. When the muzzle prevented chewing, Sandy would dig and scratch even more.

The doctor loved his dog, but he was thinking of getting rid of her. He couldn't guard Sandy for long periods every day because of the demands of his private practice. Sandy just kept getting worse. He hoped there might be some brain defect that could be treated medically, but examinations showed that Sandy was completely healthy.

As it turned out, Sandy's negative behaviors virtually disappeared within two days. Such rapid change would have been impossible if the initial cause of her problem had not been recognized. Without realizing it, the doctor had contributed to Sandy's problems. He loved her and tried to be a responsible owner, but sometimes he reinforced wrong behaviors because he misunderstood his role and Sandy's needs. He punished Sandy's normal, predictable responses to changes in her environment without considering the cause of those responses. Worst of all, the doctor did not realize how a change in his own attitudes and priorities could have such a negative impact on the dog.

Sandy had not always been destructive. At six weeks of age, Sandy was housetrained easily by the doctor and was responsive to his commands. If there was a problem at the beginning, it was that the doctor did not provide Sandy with consistent leadership. As a result, she began to act as if she was in charge. Her owner reinforced this notion by letting Sandy have her way too often. He thought permissiveness and love were synonymous.

Sandy quickly learned how to trick her owner into giving her what she wanted. She slept with him, jumped up on his lap whenever she wanted, begged successfully for table scraps, and got his attention through barking, pouting, and faking injury. She pulled on the leash during walks, not because she was a leader but because she had no one to lead her. The doctor used voice commands infrequently.

Sandy was a fairly confident dog, but she became hyperactive and insecure when she took on a leadership role. She was not a pack leader, and her instincts were more useful when a more confident dog or person took responsibility for her. Even when she pulled on the leash, she acted nervously and changed directions frequently. She lacked confidence in a leadership role, but she calmed down and displayed far more self-confidence when the doctor required her to follow him.

Since Sandy was accustomed to being the center of attention, she had trouble accepting the doctor's new fiancée. The doctor now had to split his time and loyalties, and the dog's subtle behaviors no longer worked to gain his attention. A chain reaction of negative events ensued. The owner finally remembered that Sandy began chewing the furniture shortly after his fiancée moved in with him.

Sandy became jealous when the doctor gave a lot of attention to his fiancée, so she began to compete with the woman for attention. She started to bark louder and more frequently, and she began to chew and scratch the bed because she was no longer permitted to sleep there.

The doctor used a rolled newspaper to punish the bed-chewing, but he did not realize that he was also becoming a competitive threat to Sandy. Sandy had attacked the bed only after she was banned from it. Her response to the punishment was to nip at the fiancée's ankles and to growl at her. This led to more punishment, followed by more destructive chewing.

This became a vicious cycle: Sandy and her owner were competing against each other, each one convinced the other one was wrong. The muzzle added to the conflict, so Sandy became more reactive and destructive. She began to bark and howl constantly, and her chewing became more purposeful.

The doctor could no longer trust Sandy, and he felt he could not leave her home alone. He would come home every day anticipating more destruction, and his negative emotions upon entering the house were additional competition and punishment for the dog. Instead of his usual warm, friendly greeting, he would glare at Sandy and ask her what she had done wrong that day. In essence, the doctor was punishing Sandy for coming to the door to greet him.

Out of desperation, the doctor decided to protect his furniture by locking Sandy in the bathroom while he was gone. He thought isolation would solve the problem, but it made Sandy's problem worse. When the doctor got home that day, he discovered Sandy had ripped the toilet seat off its hinges and had shredded the bathroom carpet.

At this point, many people would consider euthanasia. Fortunately, the doctor sought professional help and had the maturity to accept responsibility for his contributions to Sandy's problems. His own attitude adjustment had such a profound effect that Sandy's behavior improved almost instantly.

This is what Sandy's owner learned:

1. In the absence of neurological disorders, there is a reason for every behavior change.
2. It is necessary to understand a dog's basic survival needs and to help it satisfy these needs daily if we love it.
3. There is a difference between what a dog needs and what it wants. A dog must fulfill its needs, but if we always let it get what it wants, we are letting the dog be in charge. Excessive permissiveness is submission rather than love.

4. Most dogs prefer having people as their leaders. They are more relaxed and behaviorally sound when their owners provide consistent leadership and respect.

5. Dogs perceive as selfish and competitive people who think only of their own needs and neglect their dog's needs, and dogs will respond in like manner.

6. When we punish a dog because we are frustrated by the problems it causes us, we are competing, not showing love. To punish a dog for his normal responses to threats to his survival increases that threat.

7. If we behave in a trustworthy manner, we will also be able to trust our dogs.

8. Since not all people are natural leaders, we can help our dogs by learning how to be better leaders. We can cause great harm for our dogs, and ultimately for ourselves, by ignoring our leadership responsibilities.

9. Dogs are much smarter about fulfilling their needs than many people realize, and they are highly aware of and responsive to changes in human attitudes and emotions.

At first, the doctor saw only one side of the picture, but once he discovered the reasons for Sandy's behavior he was able to correct the situation. The doctor knew he would have to compromise so Sandy would know she was loved and was not being replaced by his fiancée. He allowed Sandy to sleep with him again and he allotted some playtime with Sandy each day.

The usual two or three daily walks were used to practice simple command-response training, a good way to establish the leader-follower relationship that Sandy needed so badly. With a confident leader at her side, Sandy could relax, and her self-confidence increased. Behaviors that arise from frustration and insecurity are less likely when self-confidence is increased.

The doctor also changed his attitude toward Sandy's selfishness. He had seen how Sandy became more hyperactive and nervous when he gave into her tricks. When he realized that Sandy thought she had dominated him, that made him much wiser.

Sandy was really a submissive dog. She did have some dominant instincts, so he didn't try to prevent all dominant behaviors, but he provided these opportunities at his own suggestion. Sandy was a lap dog, so he invited her onto his lap a couple of times each day. He permitted this only when she was not begging for it. He let Sandy think she was dominant by being on top of him, but he demonstrated his own dominance by making these episodes his decision and not Sandy's.

The doctor was stern with Sandy when necessary, but he remembered to submit and reassure her when she complied with his orders. He stopped supplementing a balanced diet with table scraps because he knew Sandy would gain too much weight through begging. This was a responsibility of his leadership, and Sandy responded positively.

Sandy's behavior improved permanently, and the doctor enjoyed his dog more than ever before. This reward is possible with an interrelationship based on understanding and mutual trust.

Whenever we become involved in a vicious cycle of competition with our dog, it's easy to forget how much our feelings and attitudes toward the dog have changed over time. Since we are helping perpetuate this negative cycle, we must accept equal blame for the problems that arise.

Once a problem begins, every behavior change that occurs afterward is a secondary complication of the chain reaction. When this cycle is broken, the pattern of negative behaviors stops, too. We must be wise enough to forget about the chain reaction and remember the good times before the cycle started. Our dogs will stop blaming us, so we should stop blaming them. When we hold a grudge against a dog, we perpetuate the vicious cycle.

Forget about the chain reaction, but try to remember the situation that may have started the negative cycle. Analyze the entire relationship you have with your dog and look for common ground on which to build a stronger relationship. Consider what you might have done wrong, from your dog's perspective, and look for better alternatives. We cannot expect a dog to change its natural tendencies just to suit us. As leaders, we must be the ones to adapt and compromise. That does not mean we should tolerate destructiveness, but we should make an effort to modify our lifestyle enough to help our dogs feel comfortable.

Don't become emotionally upset when your dog makes a mistake. Our own negative emotions sometimes prevent us from behaving in a proper manner and they have a definite negative effect on how our dogs perceive us. Instead of reacting emotionally, sit down, relax, and pay attention to what your dog is doing and why.

Put yourself in your dog's place. How would you react in similar circumstances? How would you respond to distrust or isolation? What changes would improve the situation? Try to see yourself from your dog's perspective, to enhance understanding.

Another important consideration is the difference between short-term and long-term solutions. Most people want their dogs to enjoy a long life as family members. An effort should be made to enhance a long-term relationship. Solutions to behavior problems based on short-term goals may create long-term complications.

The doctor who isolated Sandy in the bathroom was concerned only with a short-term need to protect his furniture. Did he really expect to keep Sandy locked in the bathroom forever? He probably never thought that far ahead. After only one day, isolation had an adverse effect on Sandy's behavior, and it became obvious that this was definitely not a long-term solution.

Dogs sometimes act like they are starving and they beg for extra food and treats. If the dog is receiving a well-balanced diet and is maintaining its proper weight, then we are wrong to reinforce the begging. If we give in, the extra food can cause obesity and its physical problems. The dog might also beg more frequently and act as if it is the boss. Such an erroneous perception almost always leads to additional negative behaviors.

To develop a long-term relationship, we must occasionally make some short-term sacrifices. A dog that isn't given extra treats when it begs may act hateful toward us, but this is temporary and will stop as soon as the dog accepts our decision.

Just smile and ignore the pouting because you know you are helping the dog. In the long run, the dog will benefit from your consistent leadership.

We often get angry when our dog makes mistakes, but how often do we reward it when it behaves well? Positive reinforcement through praise and petting encourages a dog to repeat its behavior. Even the worst dogs do some things right. We should make an effort to acknowledge and reinforce good behaviors. If we tell a dog what it *cannot* do, we must also tell it what it *can* do.

Since dogs are quick to notice changes in our attitudes and emotions, behavior problems arise when we let outside pressures affect us. This was the case with a two-year-old mixed breed male named Fritz.

Fritz had lived happily with its two owners since it was a puppy. Fritz was well-behaved except for a few minor problems during mating seasons. When the wife became pregnant and the husband started having problems with his employers, that had an adverse effect on Fritz.

The pressures of the pregnancy and the job problems caused Fritz's owners to neglect him. They didn't intend to harm Fritz, but they were preoccupied with other thoughts and problems. As a result, they stopped playing with Fritz and were suddenly less willing to let him get up on their laps.

Fritz sensed his owners were competing against him and he responded competitively. He urinated on the woman's leg while she washed the dishes, and he defecated on the man's favorite chair. In dog language, Fritz was utilizing more overt techniques to reinforce his own dominant instincts. While these new behaviors were irritating to his owners, Fritz finally got their attention.

The owners realized that they were unwittingly taking their problems out on their dog. While they had many decisions to make, they also knew Fritz was a part of their family and needed their leadership. They forced themselves to forget their problems long enough to give Fritz daily attention and to let him be himself. They remembered to play with him and let him up onto their laps a couple of times each day. As soon as they adopted a more positive attitude, Fritz stopped his negative behaviors and in so doing, helped prevent his owners from letting outside pressures get them down.

Most dogs have fairly equal mixtures of dominant and submissive instincts, but a few dogs are extremely submissive and a few others are extremely dominant. It takes special attitudes and considerations to interact successfully with these animals.

The owners of Barclay, a one-year-old male beagle were overly permissive and naive. They thought dogs were too dumb to know what they were doing, and too small and fragile to be ordered around by a dominant leader. As a result, Barclay could run free in the house and had never been housetrained. He urinated anywhere he wanted to, stole food, growled to scare off his owners, and bit them whenever he didn't get his way. To make matters worse, Barclay's owners thought they had no choice but to accept his behavior.

Like a spoiled child, Barclay had been pushing his owners to see how much he could get away with. They were afraid of him and fearful for him, so when they finally decided something had to be done, they had no idea how to improve the situation. They knew, though, that they wouldn't tolerate these same behaviors in their own child.

The typical pet dog behaves much like a young child. Most are easily spoiled and will try to gain dominance in the home until the owners assert themselves.

This was a revelation for Barclay's owners. One quick backhand to the muzzle when he tried to bite ended Barclay's spoiled brat days permanently. The punishment was not hard enough to cause pain, but it gained Barclay's respect. He suddenly wanted to follow his owners everywhere and seemed grateful to find good leaders.

The couple realized they had to learn more about leadership, so they practiced the leader-follower relationship with Barclay at an obedience training class. Barclay learned quickly from then on. He must have known about housetraining all along because he went outside to urinate shortly after he was slapped, and he continued to do so. Although the owners had to slap at first to stop his growling, stealing, and biting, in a short time, a simple "No!" was enough to stop his negative behaviors.

Barclay's behavior improved quickly because of the major change in his owners' attitudes. Their initial adjustment was to seek consultation and obedience training. They also had to accept the leadership role they had previously avoided and they had to face the reality of Barclay's behavior. This major adaptation was difficult for them at first, but their short-term sacrifice paid long-term dividends.

Some people have trouble believing that dogs have reasons for their behaviors. What dogs may lack in intelligence, they make up for with instinctive alertness. Some people doubt they can modify their own personality enough to help their dogs. If that is true, how can we expect our dogs to do something we cannot do?

There are many cases where a dog's behavior has changed in response to the attitude changes of its owners. If we refuse to accept responsibility for behaviors that we cause, we will have trouble correcting those behaviors. Not all dog behavior problems are caused by people, but we should always consider the possibility.

Attitude adjustment can have a profound effect on behavior change. Even if you are skeptical, try it. You may be pleasantly surprised by the results.

Chapter 9

TALKING WITH DOGS

We can communicate a great deal with dogs without ever speaking a single word. Many of us have not had much practice reading a dog's nonverbal cues because we depend so heavily on the spoken word for communication. Dogs understand our body language, confidence levels, emotions, and attitudes better than we do. But how well do they understand our language and thought patterns?

Dogs recognize certain words through repetition. They learn to associate commands with specific desired behaviors by practicing command-response training with their owners. This imprinting is as effective with words as it is with actions and sounds. Dogs learn to anticipate food when they hear us open the refrigerator door if we do this consistently before we feed them. They can also learn specific words if we use them consistently and frequently.

This is the extent to which many scientists believe dogs can understand our language. Under certain circumstances, however, some dogs appear to understand much more. It is possible to use language to improve our relationship with dogs, if we use it properly.

Whether a dog understands our language or not, it can recognize subtle differences in voice intonation. Even if it doesn't know our words, a dog can understand what we mean by listening to our tone of voice. If we mean what we say, our attitudes and confidence levels will also be reflected.

Our voices can be loud or soft, warm or cold, happy or sad, loving or hateful, high-pitched or low-pitched, confident or fearful. Dogs recognize soft, high-pitched voices as submissive, and loud, low-pitched ones as dominant. They are attracted to happy, confident, warm, and loving voices, and are repelled by sad, fearful, cold, and hateful voices. Voice intonation is nearly as important as body language in helping a dog know how to react to us.

95

The most important aspect of talking with dogs is to be truthful and to mean what we say. Dogs understand the essence of what we say by the combination of voice intonation, body language, and attitude associated with our verbal comments. If we lie, our body language and tone of voice may give us away because they are the most truthful aspects of our communication. If we make a conscious effort to speak truthfully, our nonverbal cues will accurately reflect that.

When we need to give a dog a dominant command, we should lower our voice and use simple one-word or one-phrase commands. We must have the personal confidence to feel dominant. If not, our voice will reflect a more submissive attitude that a dog can perceive readily. If it is dominant, it will probably not comply with our command. If we mean to be dominant, the dog will recognize our dominance and obey us.

When we want to praise a dog for obeying us, we should show a more submissive tone of voice by raising the pitch and offering praise honestly and with encouragement. We should act the same toward overly fearful, submissive dogs. If a dog responds to a stimulus by hiding, shaking, or submissive wetting, we should speak softly and with a higher pitch to coax it out of its excessive fear. Speaking loudly to a fearful dog increases its fears and is counterproductive. We need to find a range of voice intensity that is compatible with our dog's needs.

A truly dominant, independent dog will respect us more and stay closer to us if we speak to it as if it were an independent adult person. If we need to dominate it for bathing, grooming, or taking it to the veterinarian, we should speak to it truthfully and with respect. We can say, "You're a proud dog and I don't wish to hurt you, but I would appreciate your cooperation. I will help you if you help me." If we mean what we say and recognize the dog's right to exist as an independent being, it will understand us well enough to comply more readily with our wishes.

We must spend extra time and use compassionate words when we have a fearful dog. Crouch down to its level to appear less dominant and approach it slowly, with arms out and palms up. Use a soft, warm, loving voice and say something like, "You don't have to be afraid of me. I will protect you, and I promise not to harm you. I am your friend and I understand. You are a good dog and there is nothing to fear." People who do not understand or accept an animal who has excessive fears will never be able to provide truthful reassurance by this method because their voices will give away their true attitudes.

Spoiled dogs usually respond to statements like, "I'm on to your games. You have gotten away with your biting and tricks far too long. I won't let you trick me again. Do you understand?" Since we know a dog can become self-destructive when it is spoiled, we can look a dog directly in the eye and smile as we speak. We know we are helping the dog in the long run, so our confident tone of voice will help it understand that we mean what we say. The dog will soon forget if we are inconsistent and permit it to become indirectly dominant over us again. Actions always speak louder than words; we must prove that we mean what we say by synchronizing our actions and our words.

We should never use baby talk to a dog, that is a sure sign of submission. It indicates that the person is incapable of leadership. Since dogs and people all suffer when dogs are leaders in the home, we should control our overly submissive tendencies.

When we are responsible for the dog's problems in the home, we should apologize directly to the dog. Our voices should indicate that we are truly sorry for our errors. We expect a dog to submit to us when it is wrong, so we should do the same when we are at fault. This demonstrates to the dog that the rules we impose on it apply to us also. This improves a dog's security by helping it realize it lives in a fair environment with no double standards. We can set a good example for the dog to mimic when we obey our own rules. When we recognize our own mistakes, we can learn to improve our own behavior, which helps us and the dog.

Perhaps the most important thing we can say to a dog is, "I love you." If we truly mean it, our voice will sound warm, reassuring, happy, confident, and loving. There is no doubt then that the dog will understand us. It will be attracted to our

97

attitude because it wants and needs our love, and it will show its love for us in return. If we don't really love our dog, we are better off saying nothing. If we don't mean what we say, the dog will recognize our true feelings.

Dogs are often gullible because they really want to follow and believe us. At first, we can fake attitudes and lie in order to trick our dog into behaving certain ways. Over time, the dog will begin to doubt us if our contrived attitudes do not accurately reflect our true feelings. Ultimately, it will stop trusting us. When this happens, the dog will suffer emotionally because it has no trustworthy leader to guarantee its security and survival. Lies may work for a while, but in the long run, they almost always backfire.

Beyond Reflexes?

Dogs respond reflexively to changes in our voice intonation, body language, attitudes, and confidence levels, so it appears that they understand much of what we say. Some people believe dogs are capable of much more. We should test our dogs to see if this is true.

If we are skeptical and think dogs are dumb, we will mistakenly assume there is no understanding without ever researching other possibilities. The only way to test a dog for verbal understanding is to assume that it can understand everything we say, and then watch its body language to see what it does not understand.

A few dogs, particularly on certain "good days," appear to be capable of understanding a great deal. Some people see these dogs as people who think they are dogs. Certain behavior problems have shown immediate improvement after "heart-to-heart talks" with their owners. One dog was urinating in the house despite adequate housetraining. There was much turmoil in the home at the time; the dog's owner had many personal problems that affected his attitude and actions. These problems created territorial competition, and the dog responded by using waste marking to establish territory within the home.

The owner realized that a misunderstanding had occurred. He sat down with his dog and told it, "I love you and I want you to live with me. I'm sorry I've been too busy and frustrated to consider your needs lately, and I'll try to improve, but I cannot let you live with me if you're going to urinate in the house. If you make any more messes in the house, I'll have to get rid of you." The man meant what he said, and the dog seemed to understand because it went outside to urinate immediately and caused no additional problems inside the house. The man also improved his attitude to prevent future competition.

Selfish, spoiled dogs may not want to hear what we say if it is different from what they prefer to believe. Fearful dogs may not believe there is nothing to fear no matter what we say, because they are too nervous and hyperactive. Dominant dogs will refuse to obey our orders even if they understand every word we say, but at least some of these dogs show that they do understand.

A spoiled dog may act totally ignorant if we tell it we've caught onto its tricks. This dog is accustomed to gaining dominance through indirect methods and may not wish to change its attitude spontaneously. It may tilt its head and look at us questioningly, as if we make no sense whatsoever. But say the words which represent the dog's desired goals in a soft monotone when it is resting and apart from us and it may jump excitedly to attention. Spoiled dogs, even in the absence of specific body language and voice intonation, seem to understand a great deal when they wish to do so.

Dominant dogs refuse to obey our orders so readily that they may do the exact opposite of what we command. This makes it easy for us to test them for verbal understanding. If we order a dominant dog to do something and it does the exact opposite, then we know it must understand us pretty well.

There is another type of communication which a few highly credible people describe as an ability to communicate mentally with dogs and other living things. They describe "talking" with dogs about their lifestyles, preferences, and feelings. Some of these people, as a result of interactions with animals, have described highly specific occurrences that could have been known only by the animals and their owners.

We would be foolish to totally refuse to examine this possibility. Until recently, little research had been conducted in this area. Many people believe dogs are dumb, incapable of complex thought processes, but there is practically no research to make a definite conclusion. One thing is true: we will never research mental telepathy accurately if we refuse to admit that it is possible.

Dogs probably respond only reflexively to verbal communication, but if dogs understand everything we say, think, and feel, this might help dogs that must live with people survive better. They smell and hear far better than we do; we see better and think more analytically. Dogs seem better able to read minds; perhaps we have lost our ability to use mental telepathy as we have become more dependent on the written and spoken word. Maybe dogs don't need to read, write, or speak because they can survive without these communication techniques. Mental telepathy might be the answer.

This is not an attempt to prove the existence of mental telepathy, but since it is widely believed that dogs and people have the same origins, and since we are quite similar to dogs internally, if not externally, there could be some sort of universal language based on these similarities. If we refuse to keep an open mind, we will never know the truth. If some people can communicate mentally with dogs, maybe we all can. If there is another way we can communicate with our dogs, we should learn what it is, to improve the interaction between dogs and people.

Chapter 10

SEXUAL IMPLICATIONS

A dog's sexual behavior is often misunderstood and ignored. To a dog, sex is neither dirty or especially amorous, but is a strong, normal, instinctive drive. If we could discuss the subject objectively, we could solve many behavior problems.

Normal Sexual Behavior

Female dogs have two heat cycles a year. Each one lasts about one month. Blood drips from the vagina for the first eight to ten days of each cycle, and that, plus a changed urine smell, can attract males from great distances. Around ten-to-twelve days into the cycle, ovulation occurs. At this time, a female is most likely to accept sexual mounting from a male and is most likely to become pregnant.

Different female dogs may respond differently to the onset of their heat cycles, but all will show some behavior variations at this time. A submissive female may become extra fearful because it senses a further loss of self-control as its sexual drive becomes stronger. A more dominant female may become somewhat aggressive, may try to dart outside, or may just wish to be left alone.

Most females have heat periods in the spring and fall, so these times can be considered mating seasons. A heat cycle can occur any time of year, however. This is why some male dogs are conscious of their sexual drives all year long especially in urban areas where there are many dogs. Since they can sense a female in heat from even a great distance, male dogs are not necessarily limited to two cycles per year.

Like females, different male dogs may behave differently during sexual arousal, but no dog remains unaffected by hormonal changes. Fearful male dogs may act even more nervous when they sense a female in heat. They may be confused by

101

their own changed drives and may refuse food, stand in a corner, and shake. This is typical behavior for submissive male dogs, and many of their owners fear they are ill and check with their veterinarians. With the possible exception of a swollen prostate gland, these dogs usually have no physical problems.

It is more common for male dogs to become more arrogant as a result of their sexual drives. Aggressiveness, territorial urine markings, and the desire to roam increase. These dogs may not eat as much because they would rather dominate a female than food. Dominant instincts become so strong that these dogs may sexually mount other animals, people, or furniture in a constant attempt to receive sexual and tactile gratification. They have such a one-track mind during mating season that they may run right into the path of a moving automobile without looking or waiting if necessary. Male dogs are much more prone to accidents like this during mating season than between seasons.

Several male dogs may run more or less together during mating season because they are all looking for the same females. They will urinate and defecate on the yards and porches of homes where there are female dogs in heat. Territorial competition becomes so strong that male dogs may fight each other over which one gets the female.

We should understand that dominant male dogs think about things other than their owners when sexually aroused during the mating season. For example, a bachelor is his dog's leader between mating seasons, but during sexual arousal, the dog develops so much extra dominance that it temporarily takes over leadership. It may be well-behaved and obey all the bachelor's orders even without a leash under normal circumstances, but the dog may refuse to obey orders at this time. If it has the choice of submitting to its owner or running off to dominate a female, it will choose the latter. It may even fight back when the owner tries to pet its shoulders or otherwise dominate it. Even experienced obedience trainers have trouble controlling sexually intense male dogs. Neutering, or the end of mating season, can readjust the leadership ladder to improve dog-owner compatibility.

A male dog must dominate a female in order to mate with it. If the female is more dominant, mating will not occur since the female may chase off the male through biting, growling, or sitting down. Some females are quite promiscuous and will permit frequent matings with several males. Other females may stand for sexual mounting only during ovulation, when one or more matings often guarantees pregnancy.

After a few minutes of copulation, both male and female genitalia will swell, and they will be locked in the mating position. This normal phenomenon is commonly called a "tie," and it usually lasts for twenty to thirty minutes. The pair cannot be separated until the swelling subsides, and a male frequently will turn around (as if to run away) so that the two dogs appear end-to-end. This locking process has a survival advantage in that it keeps the sperm inside the vagina to help insure pregnancy and therefore species survival.

Many people panic when they see a pair of dogs tied in the mating position and try to break them up. They may hit them or throw water on them, but that only makes matters worse. Excess pressure can damage both the penis and the vagina. You cannot prevent pregnancy by pulling them apart anyway, so it is better to wait until relaxation permits a natural separation. There are medications veterinarians give within the first week after mating to prevent pregnancy.

Some owners leave their ovulating female dogs outside where they are most likely to attract males. This is a bad idea if mating is not desired because dogs will follow their normal instinctive drives whether we want them to or not. Some people have caught and killed male dogs mounting their females, but this is completely unjustified. It is not the dogs who are to blame, but the people who give dogs a sexual opportunity too convenient to ignore.

A dog's normal pregnancy lasts an average of sixty-three days. Healthy pups can be born anytime between fifty-eight and sixty-eight days following mating. There are behavior changes during pregnancy, especially during the last few weeks. It is common for an expectant mother to be irritable and restless as the abdomen enlarges, so it may be a good idea to keep her away from small children. In the last week of pregnancy, the pregnant bitch may seek seclusion, carry toys around in her mouth, and soil the floors. She may also shred papers, blankets, and cloth materials to use as a nest for her pups. She will stop eating abruptly.

We should leave the bitch alone once she has started labor. She is going to be taking hormonal orders from her pups and may resent our interference. It is important not to move or irritate the female once abdominal contractions have started. Even if she has taken a beautiful, expensive bedspread as a whelping area, if you move her she can go out of labor and have negative complications. A dog's normal instincts usually guarantee a successful birth with no need for human intervention.

Problems with People

We cause many sexual behavior problems when we misunderstand the basic realities of a dog's sexual instincts. Unknowingly, we reinforce male and female dogs to continue behaviors which ultimately cause problems for the dogs and for us. Many of these problems perpetuate themselves simply because many people are unwilling or unable to understand the situation. Many people compound the problem by refusing to discuss it openly with their veterinarians or with each other.

Bobby, a three-year-old male bull terrier, had been urinating in the house to mark territory for more than two years. The owners tolerated this behavior because Bobby would only urinate when they were gone. They had taken him to obedience school, but he was too strong-willed to obey orders.

Since he was not allowed outside, Bobby found another way to satisfy his strong sexual drives. The owners finally admitted that Bobby substituted balls, toys, pillows, and furniture for the girlfriend he needed. Bobby would masturbate for hours at a time, by massaging his genitals on these objects. He was so strong-willed that he was the leader in the home, and the owners were afraid to try and stop him from behaving this way.

104

The owners permitted Bobby to reinforce his dominant instincts and sexual drives so often that he became preoccupied by them. The more reinforcement he received, the more he would urinate in the house. This was a vicious cycle and the owners were convinced there was nothing they could do to change the dog's behavior.

A two-year-old male German shepherd named Rip was unable to leave the house so it substituted the wife in the family for a female dog. The husband noticed that the dog was hyperactive during mating season and would pace back and forth and pant at the front door. He also noticed that his wife was overly loving toward Rip and allowed him to approach her sexually.

The wife was asked to describe Rip's behavior. She said she felt that the dog loved her more and needed her attention because her husband didn't like to play with the dog. She said that sometimes Rip would wet on her arm or leg. Actually, Rip would mount her arm or leg and then ejaculate on her. Her husband knew what Rip was doing, but she refused to believe there were any sexual implications.

Unfortunately, the husband was proved right because one day, the wife was busy and she declined Rip's advances. Rip was so accustomed to satisfying his sexual needs with the woman that he knocked her to the floor. He growled and bit at her and forced her to lay still until he had ejaculated on her. A male with this strong a sexual drive doesn't see much difference between a female dog and human female. As long as there is sexual reinforcement, there is behavioral repetition that worsens over time.

Many girls just reaching puberty are bitten by male dogs each year. Male dogs can detect these physical changes readily and are often attracted to the girls. Since children often get down on their knees to play and wrestle with dogs, it is not uncommon for male dogs to show dominant mounting behaviors toward them. If a male dog has been reinforced to mount a young girl, it will be especially interested in mounting her once she has reached puberty. She probably doesn't realize that she may be reinforcing the dog's notion that she is his sexual partner. If she tries to push the dog away during mounting, it may bite her.

We must see the reality of a dog's sexual behavior in order to know what not to reinforce. We also need to understand that it is normal for dogs to be more sexually uninhibited than we are. Regardless of our personal preferences, we should not expect our dogs to change their behavior simply to perpetuate our own sensitivities.

It is not uncommon for people to lock their dogs out of their bedrooms when they are making love. There is no reason to do this, and a dog's behavioral reaction is not always acceptable. A dog may urinate and defecate on the floor next to the bedroom door to claim territory it cannot otherwise claim.

Some dogs are permitted to sleep in bed between a man and a woman. This may encourage the dog to want close physical contact with one or both parties. These dogs are sometimes even permitted to rub or lick human genitalia. Whether we wish to believe it or not, such situations do occur. There is nothing wrong with letting a dog sleep on the bed as long as it cannot come between husband and wife or share excessive sexual or emotional rewards.

The Value of Neutering

The only totally successful way to control a dog's sexual behaviors is to neuter it. Some people mistakenly believe that a female dog has to reproduce at least once to be healthy. Actually, pregnancy in many ways is a disease when you consider all the physical and emotional changes that occur. The massive hormonal changes that occur twice a year during the mating seasons place a severe stress on any dog. Since there are so many more dogs than there are people willing to care for them, neutering helps prevent a worsening of the overpopulation problem.

Many people believe male dogs should be permitted to roam freely to seek sexual gratification. Some even say male dogs should be able to do all the things they themselves cannot do.

But free-running male dogs cause many public health problems and are often involved in car accidents. A male dog's sexual drives are reduced only temporarily when he has a female to mate with, so this is not a good solution, either.

A surgical spay (ovariohysterectomy) removes a female's ovaries and uterus. Surgical removal of a male's testes is called castration. Despite old wives' tales to the contrary, these surgical procedures offer many benefits and few, if any, problems.

There are behavioral and health reasons for neutering dogs. We know dogs benefit from stable home environments and from an opportunity to balance their instinctive needs. Neutering helps eliminate the sometimes extreme confidence level changes that occur during mating seasons for females and throughout the year for males. It permits dogs to remain balanced emotionally which also gives their owners the opportunity to maintain a leadership role at all times. Many other behavior problems are less common in neutered animals as well because there are fewer leadership ladder changes. Neutered dogs may still be conscious of mating seasons, but they are not bothered as much by them.

Neutering a female dog prevents the blood spotting at the beginning of heat cycles plus all the problems created around the home by male dogs that are roaming. It allows a female dog to look to its owners for leadership rather than seek it from male dogs or from its own puppies. Fearful females may actually gain confidence through neutering and may no longer show the complete loss of confidence that sometimes occurs during heat periods.

Castration offers many behavioral benefits for male dogs. It reduces his desire to roam, howl, pace, scratch at the door, and to set up territory in the home with urine marking. It eliminates sexual mounting, masturbation, and aggressive biting so easily reinforced in non-neutered males. It reduces arrogance to a more relaxed confidence level that indicates stability and balance. Castrated male dogs are more likely to accept owner leadership and obedience training, and fearful males may become more confident, no longer troubled by the stresses of hormonal change.

Many male dogs are not extremely aggressive during sexual arousal, but their attention is divided nonetheless. It is often hard for a male dog to decide between its need for people and its need for sex. If it has some fears, it may act fearfully one minute and aggressively the next. This instinctive conflict is an emotional stress for male dogs, and it reduces our ability to balance their behavior and to help fulfill their instinctive needs. Neutering changes a complex problem into a simple one and gives us the opportunity to eliminate one major instinctive need completely.

Some people worry that neutering will cause negative behavioral changes, and are especially concerned that castration might cause a feminization of male dogs. This is not true. Most behavior change associated with neutering offers specific advantages for dogs and their owners. All dogs have both male and female hormones that are produced by the adrenal glands, so neutering does not altogether eliminate sexual hormones. A few females may occasionally lose some control of their bladder if they are spayed before their first heat period, but this is not typical. Overall, most male and female dogs become much better pets after neutering.

There are also many physical reasons to consider neutering. Neutering lessens or prevents many diseases and health problems. False pregnancies are common and can occur even without sexual contact with a male. False pregnancy causes milk production, an enlarged and painful abdomen, nesting behavior, and the carrying of toys and other objects around the house. It becomes more common with age and is not beneficial to the dog's physical well-being.

Nonspayed females have a greatly increased chance of developing breast tumors. A dog spayed at six months of age (prior to its first heat period) has less than one percent chance of developing breast tumors, while one spayed immediately after its first heat has a twenty-five percent chance. The incidence of breast tumors increases with age and intact females over five years old have more than a fifty percent chance of developing them.

Tumors of the uterus and ovaries are also more common as

the dog gets older. Infections of the uterus are increasingly common in older nonspayed females with or without sexual contact, and many of these infections are life-threatening if not treated in time. The potential for these problems is eliminated with neutering.

Both males and females have greater dietary needs when they are not neutered. Some people complain that animals become obese following neutering surgery. This does not usually occur if the diet is reduced as a dog's nutritional needs diminish. Because dogs burn so much energy trying to fulfill their sexual drives, reducing total food consumption by one-third or more following neutering prevents obesity and is economically sound.

Intact dogs also have an increased likelihood of contracting disease. Any kind of stress—pregnancy, nervousness, sexual frustration, riding in a hot car—weakens the body and a dog is more susceptible to disease because it cannot fight off infections as well.

Males have as much chance as females to develop physical problems. Like their human counterparts, male dogs have prostate glands. As the prostate enlarges, a male experiences pain and constipation, has trouble urinating, and can even die. Although human prostates are routinely removed, surgical removal of a dog's prostate is difficult. Neutering effectively reduces its size and prevents future prostate enlargement.

Tumors of the prostate, testes, and tissue around the anus (perianal adenomas) are much less common after neutering. A male dog is also much less likely to develop a perineal hernia when he is neutered.

In most cases, the advantages of neutering far outweigh any potential disadvantages. With a combination of neutering, owner attitude adjustment, daily command-response training, and love, most dog behavior problems can be resolved for the benefit of dogs and their owners.

Chapter 11

COPING WITH CHANGES
IN FAMILY STRUCTURE

A dog reacts to changes in its environment. These reactions can be strong if there is a major change in the dog's home or family. Visitors, extended owner absence, a birth or death in the family, divorce, or a move to a new home can all create instinctive conflicts for a dog. This is particularly true for a dog that lacks strong, consistent leadership. Anticipation and proper preparation can help prevent adverse behavioral reactions to these major changes.

There are three different ways a dog may react to a visitor in the home. A submissive dog may run and hide out of fear, while a dominant dog may walk or run up to the intruder. A dominant dog may jump up on the visitor's legs, and it may even growl and bite at the visitor if its need to protect its territory is strong. A balanced, confident dog may take only brief notice of the visitor and then rest or return to its previous activity, especially if it has met the visitor before. A dog may behave differently toward different visitors, depending on their general attitudes and confidence levels.

Ideally, every dog should treat every visitor in a relaxed, balanced manner and not react out of extreme dominance or extreme submission. Any variation from this relaxed approach should be anticipated because it provides an excellent opportunity for us to work with our dogs and help them avoid behavioral extremes.

A dog that runs away and hides in the presence of strangers is too fearful for its own good. If we permit it to remain fearful, we reinforce hiding as proper behavior and prevent the dog from getting over its fears by learning to accept strangers comfortably. When we expect visitors, we should remember our dog's tendencies and stand by its side to provide reassurance when the visitors arrive. We should tell the dog it has nothing to fear and encourage it to come forward and meet the visitors.

It should be permitted to smell and otherwise examine the visitors in a quiet, stable environment, and nobody should walk toward it or show it sudden movements that might reinforce its fears. We should demonstrate a relaxed confidence that does not appear especially dominant or threatening, and we should praise and reassure the dog for every indication that it is less fearful.

We should do this every time there is a visitor, until the dog no longer runs away. Since we will always have visitors, a dog will be unhappy if it spends much of its time hiding. The added nervousness of that situation is a stress that can create behavior problems, and it can make a dog more susceptible to physical disease.

A dominant, aggressive dog perceives itself as head of the household. It feels a strong need to know about all territorial intruders and to run them off the property if they are competitive threats to the dog's dominance. Visitors, postal workers, meter readers and others are bitten each year because they walk onto territory claimed by dominant dogs. Many dogs are isolated from visitors to keep them from dominating. That may help in the short run, but the frustrations created for the dog may cause it to chew, dig, or scratch excessively and thus create greater long-term problems.

Dominant dogs need an opportunity to check out visitors, but we must fulfill our leadership responsibilities on a daily basis so the dog doesn't become overly dominant in the home. We must develop a consistent enough relationship so we can induce a dog to obey us when there are visitors, without any need for isolation.

When we expect visitors, we should be prepared to pet the dog and hold it if necessary to keep it from attacking or otherwise dominating. We should be good enough leaders to induce compliance without punishment. We should tell the dog that these are our friends, we do not want to run them off, and that everything will be all right because we are there to control the situation. We should not let the dog jump up on visitors or growl at them. If the dog reacts strongly to every visitor, it might be helpful to schedule guests on a regular basis simply to practice our approach and to reassure the dog that visitors will come and go with no major changes or problems. If we are good leaders, our dogs will obey us.

It is important to tell visitors if our dogs tend to behave aggressively. "Beware of Dog" signs can protect them from the bite wounds they might receive if they intrude on the dog's property. We should encourage our friends and relatives not to tolerate overly dominant behavior by the dog. Letting it jump up on visitors may reinforce it to jump up on us and future visitors on a more regular basis. If we praise the dog when it relaxes and accepts visitors without dominance or fear, we encourage it to repeat its positive behavior.

When an owner must be away from home longer than usual, this can disrupt a dog's regular schedule. If it is well-adjusted, it will not suffer or cause problems in the home during these extended absences. Several precautions can help reduce problems.

It is helpful to talk to the dog before you leave home. Whether or not it understands what we say, the dog may be more relaxed during our absence if we reassure it that we love it, that we will be home eventually, and that there is nothing to worry about. It is important to speak with confidence and reassurance because any anxiousness or worry will be reflected in our voices and will cause the dog undue concern. We should let the dog know that we trust it not to disobey, and that it can trust us to return.

If we are concerned that the dog may become excessively hungry or have trouble controlling urine and bowel movements by having to change its daily schedule, we can ask a friend to come into the home during our absence to tend to the dog's needs. This person should be well known to the dog and shouldn't alarm it by entering the home unexpectedly. The friend should have several opportunities to interact with the dog in our presence so it will accept the friend and not consider the visits unusual. We may need to find a good kennel or alternative home site if we must be gone for several days at a time.

If a dog is spoiled and expects its owner to be home at all

times, or if it has become excessively dependent on the owner for attention and close contact, an extended absence can cause it to worry and overreact. It is a good idea to practice leaving and returning so if we must suddenly be away for several hours at a time, the dog will know that when we leave, we will return.

We can start by leaving for fifteen minutes. When we return, we should praise the dog and show it love for waiting for us without behavioral overreaction. Then we can gradually spend longer amounts of time away from home, and each time return with praise for the dog. When we have to be away all day, the dog will wait more patiently because it knows we will return eventually.

When we move to a new home it can be traumatic for the dog, but it doesn't have to be. We can prepare it to make the drastic change by conditioning it to the new home before we move in and by considering its needs during the move. We should reassure the dog that the home belongs as much to it as to the other family members.

On moving day, we should act like it is no different from any other day. If we ignore or isolate the dog during the move, it may think we are leaving without it. We should talk reassuringly to the dog and portray a happy confidence that indicates pleasure rather than fear or anxiety. Anticipation and prevention are crucial in helping a dog accept the home change without undue trauma to its emotional stability.

Changes in family structure can also have a negative effect on a dog. Every addition or subtraction changes the organization of the family's leadership ladder, and a dog may either gain or lose confidence at this time. Consider the effects of the birth of a new baby, the later adoption of a pet cat, and the birth of a second child on a dog without strong adult leadership and only modest confidence levels.

The addition of two new babies and a cat makes the dog lose much confidence and finds itself lower on the leadership ladder. A dog usually perceives a new baby as the new pack leader. The baby cries and its parents come running. That tells the dog that its owners are now obeying orders from the baby. At the same time, a wife's confidence is sometimes improved when she completes a successful pregnancy and a husband's confidence may be reduced. The wife is reinforced by having fulfilled her maternal instincts, while the husband is forced to accept a more subordinate role in family priorities.

The later addition of a dominant, supremely confident cat can place the husband and dog even lower on the leadership ladder. A confident cat will often try to dominate the person in the family who is most competitive for leadership, so this cat tries to sleep on top of or otherwise dominate the new baby. As the cat becomes pack leader, the other family members lose a little confidence relative to the cat.

Children lose some of their early confidence when they are no longer permitted to get their way all the time. They lose even more confidence when a new baby enters the home and starts giving orders. The first child may become competitive with its mother when the second child is born, as the cat competes against the second child. The husband and dog have lost even more confidence and now compete against each other not to be last in the pecking order. The loser may suffer emotionally and physically. If the dog loses, it may demonstrate submissive behavior problems, run away from home, or even lose the will to live.

Every change in confidence level can also change behavior, so the key to helping a dog during these changes in family size and structure is to help it maintain its initial confidence level. If we anticipate possible repercussions before these changes take place, we can give the dog the reassurance it needs to help it maintain its balance. We must then continue to consider the dog's needs and not let other family members distract us from fulfilling our leadership responsibilities to the dog. We can best help the dog during family changes by considering that its survival needs are equal to, but not greater or less than, those of all other family members.

A dog can also suffer from the trauma of divorce or a death in the family. This is particularly true if it had a stronger attachment to the departed member than to others in the family. Whenever these traumatic changes occur, we should never overlook the possibility that the dog may suffer, and we should continue to consider the dog's needs. If it received most of its love, attention, and physical contact from the person who is no longer present, these needs must now be met by the rest of the family.

Some dogs become extremely depressed by the loss of a loved one. It can be as physically and emotionally difficult for a dog as for a person. These situations are bound to arise, but if we consider what our dog is feeling, we can help it by substituting ourselves for the departed family member. If we become adequate surrogates, most dogs are able to successfully survive the temporary hardship of the sudden loss of love.

Chapter 12

THE SPECIAL PROBLEMS OF CHILDREN

Understanding the realities of dog behavior is more difficult for children than for adults. Children also have a short attention span and find it hard to accept responsibility, yet many people acquire a dog in order to satisfy the needs and wants of their children and expect them to be totally responsible for the dog's welfare.

Dogs can provide children with close, warm, physical contact and companionship. It is more important for a child to have close loving contact with parents, but dogs can improve a child's emotional security. They can be valued playmates. Under the right circumstances, dogs can help fulfill many of a child's own needs, but they are not toys that can be played with, abused, and then discarded.

Since children cannot understand the responsibilities of dog ownership, people shouldn't get dogs just for their children. All family members should be willing to share these responsibilities and to keep the dog throughout its lifetime. Children often cause behavior problems for dogs by mistreating them. Many dogs are discarded or are put to sleep just because the children have become bored with them. In these cases, no thought is given to the dog's welfare.

Most children act either physically dominant or fearful. Neither condition is desirable for dogs or children. Children have a very narrow view of the world and tend to think only of themselves. If children think dogs exist just for their benefit, they are likely to ignore the dog's needs. Many children pose competitive threats to dogs when they invade their territory and try to be physically dominant (Fig. 21). They reinforce and encourage unwanted behaviors through misunderstanding.

Some children will walk right up to a dog and jump on it as if it were a rocking horse. This is an overt act of dominance that many dogs will not tolerate without a fight. Some children

Fig. 21. Some children cause problems for dogs by mishandling them.

also hit dogs with their hands or toys, especially in families where physical punishment is commonplace, and they may pull on a dog's ears, tail, and hair (Fig. 22). Only well-balanced, contented dogs with an ability to be directly submissive can tolerate this dominance without either fighting back or running away out of fear.

It is quite common for dogs to bite, growl, and snap at children who behave aggressively toward them. It is also common for a child's parents to blame the dog rather than the child when a dog defends itself. Many children are bitten by dogs that are responding to a dominant challenge. This is normal behavior for a dog with dominant tendencies, so it is usually the child's misunderstanding and improper behavior that are to blame.

Fig. 22. Dogs will defend themselves against overly aggressive children.

A five-year-old female cairn terrier was permitted to claim indirect dominance in the home. It imagined itself to be the leader in the house, but a young daughter in the family was permitted to carry it around like a teddy bear. The dog often growled and fussed whenever the child tried to dominate it, but it usually did not try to bite the girl.

One day the dog was sitting on the father's lap, and the girl came up to the dog and began to hug and pet it. The dog did not wish to be dominated while it was dominating the man, so it bit her. The family decided the dog was untrustworthy and had it destroyed. This was senseless since the problem could have been corrected through attitude adjustment. If the family had maintained a better leadership role with the dog and had taught the girl how to behave with the dog, the dog would never have bitten the child. There was nothing wrong with the dog, but it was put to sleep anyway.

Another man and woman were contemplating marriage. The man had two young children from a previous marriage and the woman owned a two-year-old female German shepherd. The dog was normally well-behaved but was affected by changes in its owner's confidence level and was somewhat fearful of strange environments. The couple decided to introduce the dog to the children since they wanted the whole group to function as a family. They were nervous and anxious about how the dog and children would get along.

The children were somewhat rowdy and they scared the dog by running at it and dominating it physically. The dog was in heat, was not accustomed to abusive treatment and the aggressive actions of children, and it was probably more nervous than usual because of its owner's anxiety. The dog growled at the children constantly and occasionally tried to nip at them. It was trying to retain its own integrity and defend its personal space, but the results of this one brief encounter convinced the man and woman that marriage was unfeasible.

There are many types of competition between children and dogs. If a child is afraid of a dog, it may keep the dog out of its bedroom or flail its arms at the dog whenever the dog approaches. If other family members accept the dog and permit it free access to the rest of the house, the dog may not understand why it cannot enter the child's bedroom as well. If it sees the child as a competitive challenge, it may urinate on the floor right next to the child's bedroom door or approach the child more frequently in order to gain dominance.

Some children give attention and love to a dog part of the time. That makes the dog depend on the child for this relationship, but the child ignores it at other times. This is typically irresponsible behavior that is commonplace in children. A four-year-old spayed female Kerry blue terrier began urinating on the floor next to the bed of the family's twelve-year-old daughter. The girl enjoyed her relationship with the dog and was its most frequent companion. When she reached puberty and had other things on her mind, she began to ignore the dog and push it away, and became a competitive challenge. To reclaim her as its own, the dog began urine marking next to her bed.

Children often reinforce incorrect behaviors in dogs. Many children either innocently or mischievously teach dogs to behave badly through their own lack of understanding. If a dog is constantly teased into aggressive responses or is encouraged to be aggressive toward other animals or people, that can reinforce dominant tendencies which can become too difficult to control. If a dog is given too many snacks, that encourages obesity, begging for food and stealing food, and it causes a dog to eliminate waste matter too frequently and inconsistently. Tug of war games can reinforce a dog's chewing and mouthing tendencies so much that it may want to play tug of war with the furniture when the child is not home. If a dog hears constant yelling, its nerves will be on edge and it may bark louder to get attention. By scolding or otherwise punishing a dog incorrectly for behaving normally, we can cause confusion, aggressiveness, or excessive fear.

Children sometimes create a dog's sexual problems. Sometimes this is accidental and sometimes it is purposeful. Regardless, stimulating a dog's erogenous zones or permitting it to engage in sexual mounting can encourage the dog to expect sexual gratification from children or other people. A dog might assume dominance over children or become dependent on them to fulfill its needs. That can lead to other behaviors such as territorial housesoiling and biting. Children should not learn the facts of life from dogs, but they should be told truthfully how their behaviors can contribute to a dog's problems.

Generally, any child can become a competitive challenge for a dog, and all children should understand how their own attitudes and behaviors can cause problems for dogs. As children get older, their confidence levels change. If at any point in this process their confidence levels match those of their dogs, competition can result. At the same time, dogs can perceive specific differences among young children, adolescents, and adults. The onset of puberty can change a dog's perception of, and behavior toward, certain children.

The birth of a new baby is often a traumatic experience for a dog. Changes in the leadership ladder often take place, and the turmoil of pregnancy and the need to prepare the home for the new baby can be perceived by a dog as a survival threat. It is easy to ignore a dog's needs at this time.

Behavior changes can be minimized if we remember to maintain as normal a relationship as possible with our dogs. If we let the dog know that we love it and will continue to value its existence and help it fulfill its needs despite the new baby, most dogs will tolerate the new arrival with few, if any, behavior changes. If we develop and maintain a mutually beneficial relationship with our dog, that prevents many problems (Fig. 23).

People who work with animals and their owners on a consistent basis have noticed that families with rowdy, spoiled children often have dogs with behavior problems. There are many similarities between children and dogs, so there are many similarities between the recommendations for handling children and for handling dogs.

The first and most important thing to remember is that the rules we create for our dogs must apply equally to our children. The double standard created by parents is a major source of conflict between dogs and children. It is amazing how many parents assume their children are always right and their dogs always wrong when problems arise, when children are often to blame. If we only blame the dog, we do both the dog and the child an injustice. If we don't reprimand a child for incorrect behavior, we perpetuate it and create a severe survival threat for the dog. No matter how perfect we think our children are, they may have to share the blame with dogs when competitive conflicts arise. It is often the dog's perspective that the child is wrong; its behavior toward the child is its instinctive reaction to what it perceives as a survival threat.

We must look objectively at the real cause of conflict between a child and a dog. If the dog goes up to a child and bites it without provocation, the dog is wrong. If the child provokes the bite through territorial intrusion, dominant behavior, or food stealing, the child is wrong and must be made to understand that.

Fig. 23. With good preparation and consistent treatment, dogs and babies can coexist without problems.

It is a good idea in these instances to reprimand the child in front of the dog. It is helpful to tell the dog, in the presence of the child, that it has a right to growl at the child for treating it badly. This lets the dog know that its needs are being considered, and it encourages the child to behave better. A child and a dog both benefit when they are treated with equal respect.

Children must be taught how to interact with and be responsible for dogs with actions as well as words. Children often treat dogs the way their parents do, so they benefit from parents who are constructive role models. They learn by watching their parents and then practicing techniques under adult supervision. They cannot do this if they are given sole responsibility for a dog's welfare.

Like dogs, children must balance their own instinctive needs. They should learn not to be overly dominant or overly submissive and fearful around dogs. If they are too dominant and aggressive, they should be taught not to invade a dog's territory and how to avoid actions which a dog might perceive as survival threats. If children are overly fearful of dogs, they should be encouraged to get over their fears and should be given opportunities for positive, loving interactions with dogs. The best way to interact with any strange dog is to stand perfectly still and neither try to approach it nor run away from it until it can inspect and smell us to determine if we are a threat. Dogs respond best when we are not overly dominant or overly submissive in their presence.

Children who are permitted to treat dogs like unbreakable toys become adults who are irresponsible dog owners. If we can teach our children about a dog's nature and how to fulfill its basic survival needs through responsible leadership, they will someday become responsible adult dog owners. The future of the human-dog relationship can be enhanced if we take positive action at the start. Dogs do so much for us; it might be nice to return the favor.

Chapter 13

INTERACTIONS WITH OTHER ANIMALS

Many people have more than one pet. There is a greater likelihood of problems when several animals live together. The possible combinations of behavior interactions is infinite when several animals live together. There are many families with several dogs and/or cats that live together harmoniously, but others compound behavior problems by adding additional animals to their households.

Some dogs discover strong natural attractions to other dogs that may have nothing to do with sexuality or reproduction. Two dogs of average confidence may form a strong enough bond between them to run together and fulfill instinctive needs together. Such a pair, sometimes called a "brace," can function as one extremely confident dog for either constructive or destructive purposes. Their teamwork can be something to behold.

Some dogs don't get along well together. Since leadership ladders are always in question, every dog constantly looks at how it compares with dogs and other animals in its environment. Disputes are always possible when two animals of similar confidence levels seek to fulfill the same instinctive needs at the same time. Two dominant dogs may fight and two submissive dogs may act jealous and use indirect methods to bother each other, all out of competition.

Dogs understand each other quite well by using a variety of communication signals. Competition always exists, not just when actual fights begin. Dogs may compete for their owner's attention, their food bowls, water, where they sleep, which one goes in and out of the door first, which one sits on the master's favorite chair, which one greets the owner at the door, and for a myriad of other reasons. If we ignore and therefore permit these minor episodes, that may cause more destructive competition. Even without extremes, the results of competition can affect the entire family's leadership ladder and can adversely affect the behavior of one or all of the competitors.

Competition Reactions between Dogs

One of the most common types of competition is two male dogs fighting over a female. This is common in many animal species and can occur even when sexual goals are not involved.

Ginger, a confident eleven-year-old neutered female cocker spaniel-dachshund mixture lives in a home with two dominant cats. Ginger has a long leash and enjoys standing at the furthest boundary of her back yard to watch other dogs and cats pass by. One of her best friends is a neighborhood cat that visits frequently. The two do not touch one another, but they sit and look at each other for long periods of time.

Ginger also enjoys visits from two male dogs that regularly walk past her territory with their owners. One male is a well-behaved Doberman pinscher named Chan and the other dog, Rex, is a mixed breed dog that looks somewhat like a German shepherd. Chan and Rex are both attracted to Ginger even though she was neutered many years before. Ginger seems to enjoy their visits a great deal.

One day, all three dogs were permitted to contact each other off leash to test their reactions to each other. In the photo sequence (Figs. 24 to 29) we can see some interesting competition. Before Ginger joined the two males, both Chan and Rex took turns urinating and rubbing their paws on ground that Ginger frequents when she is outside. They were leaving their calling cards and announcing their interest in Ginger. They smelled and circled each other, but this territorial competition was inocuous and did not provoke violent behavior.

Ginger's presence altered the situation markedly. All three dogs began to smell each other, and Ginger seemed excited to see her friends. Ginger went right up to Chan and tried to mount him. Chan was confident but directly submissive and occasionally permitted Ginger to mount him from the side and thrust her pelvis back and forth. Rex did not want this to happen and he kept walking between Chan and Ginger.

Fig. 24. Ginger smells for urine and paw oil markings while Chan smells Ginger.

Fig. 25. Ginger smells Chan's anal sacs while Rex begins to interfere.

Fig. 26. Chan gives Rex a dominant stare and growls to run him off.

Fig. 27. Chan and Rex begin to fight violently over Ginger.

Fig. 28. During a brief pause in the fight, Ginger is seen helping Chan by biting Rex in the rear.

Fig. 29. Once the fight is stopped, Chan lets Ginger dominate his head.

Ginger shoved her nose into Rex's shoulder, as if to push him away. This didn't discourage Rex, so Chan decided to take care of things himself. He walked up to Rex from the dominant right side, separated his lips to display his teeth, and glared sideways at Rex to force him to back off.

If Rex had been less dominant than Chan, he would have backed off from this dominant display. Instead, he attacked Chan, and the two began to fight violently. This seemed to be an even match, and the owners of the two males were curious to see which dog would win, but Ginger decided to help Chan against Rex. While Rex and Chan chewed on each other's cheeks, Ginger started to bite Rex's rear end area. It was obvious that Ginger preferred Chan, and the two helped each other.

After a minute or two, the owners decided to break up the fight since Rex and Chan appeared ready to actually hurt each other. Ginger ignored both dogs for a short while. Eventually she went back to Chan as Rex's owner held him tightly to keep him from resuming the fight. Chan and Ginger smelled each other briefly, then Ginger mounted Chan from the front and placed her body on top of Chan's head. Chan is more confident than Ginger, but they seem to be compatible enough so that Chan permits Ginger to dominate him on occasion.

This brief encounter teaches us some valuable lessons. Obviously, Rex and Chan would have continued to fight over a neutered female dog until one party was injured enough to walk away submissively. This type of competition is potentially too damaging to the losing dog's physical and emotional health to be permitted, if there is an alternative. There are many other instances when dogs fight only enough to test rather than hurt each other. The results help dogs accept their place in the pecking order, so there are times when simple squabbles should be permitted. People who try to break up some of these simple squabbles might be the only ones who are injured.

A prominent public official owned two intact large breed male dogs. They had a great relationship until an indirectly dominant male cocker spaniel puppy was added to the family. The puppy got the owner's attention more frequently than the other two dogs by using a number of indirect tricks, and it would get up on the owner's lap to dominate him.

This sudden shift in the leadership ladder cast the other two dogs into more subordinate roles and isolated them from the owner's attention. One day, the owner caught them fighting over last place in the rankings and tried to break them up. Neither dog was injured, but the owner got a cut on his arm that required stitches.

The two fighting dogs didn't intend to hurt each other. They were just reacting to their suddenly lowered position in the family. The situation was corrected by neutering all three dogs and then equalizing the owner's attitudes and actions toward them. Additional squabbles were successfully prevented.

There are many situations where changes in the leadership ladder occur. These changes frequently cause competitive reactions in dogs. The death of the pack leader dog may cause formerly subordinate dogs to fight for the new leadership position. If the pack leader becomes senile and loses confidence, one or more other dogs in the family may begin to compete for pack leadership. Environmental changes can provide opportunities for young dogs with increasing confidence levels to compete more successfully with older dogs.

The move to a new home is sometimes sufficient to cause leadership changes. Two fox terrier males began to compete with each other when they moved. The older dog had established its territory and position in the first home before the younger dog was acquired. The older dog successfully dominated the newcomer at first, but the change of residence gave the younger dog the opportunity to take over the leadership position.

Where the younger dog formerly submitted passively to the older dog's dominant actions, it now began to fight back successfully. The older dog didn't want to accept these changes automatically, and tried to maintain its dominance through fighting and urine marking in the new home. Without the owner's intervention, these dogs might have destroyed their new home or each other because of competition.

Overcrowding is a common reason that dogs compete depending on their confidence levels. It might be said that the fox terriers suffered from overcrowding, depending on their confidence levels. Certainly the more animals housed together, the greater the chance of overcrowding problems. One family consisted of three people, five dogs, and two cats. The many different interrelationships imposed on these animals by living together caused many behavior problems. Some families have even more animals, and such overcrowding almost always causes numerous competitive reactions.

Sometimes we have to arrange alternative housing for groups of dogs that must live together. A man who owned seventeen dogs lived in a rural area and had several fenced-off areas for his dogs. At first, he let all the dogs run together, but this was unsuccessful. Males fought each other over certain females; two male dogs united to function as one strong pack leader and began fighting other males for the females; and one dog killed another dog that wandered too close to its territory.

The owner saw that his dogs tended to split into three distinct groups, each with its own pack leader(s). He wisely divided his dogs into these three natural packs and let each pack have its own fenced area. Each group functioned as a pack and had far fewer competitive reactions.

We often cause competitive problems for dogs housed together when we favor one over the others or permit unnecessary competition. This is especially true when we favor a dog that is not perceived by the other dogs to be the pack leader, or permit the most dominant dog to excessively dominate the others. Our inequitable attitudes can cause chain reaction problems.

Consider the case of two female Pembroke Welsh Corgis named Sandy and Penny. Sandy was a year older than Penny, and both had lived with the same family since they were puppies. The dogs got along with each other reasonably well, as long as Sandy was able to dominate Penny.

The wife of the family became increasingly protective of Penny and competitive against Sandy. Sandy was the husband's favorite dog, and his preference helped perpetuate Sandy's dominance over Penny. On the other hand, the wife felt sorry for Penny and began to show specific favoritism toward her. She would punish Sandy whenever she used her normal dominant tendencies against Penny. She began to offer Penny extra treats, attention, and time on her lap, while she refused Sandy's advances. This provoked jealous reactions in Sandy.

The favoritism and unequal treatment from the husband and wife made Sandy begin to lose confidence. Penny began to gain confidence until their confidence levels were just about equal. At this point, there was inevitable competition and fighting.

Whenever two or more dogs live together, competition is always a possibility. Some competition should be permitted since dogs have a natural instinctive need to determine their places in the leadership ladder. The best way to prevent negative or destructive competitive reactions is to treat all dogs equally. If one dog gets a treat, all dogs should receive the same treat. If we play with one dog, we should remember to provide equal time for all the dogs.

We should determine the order of the leadership ladder and permit these relationships to exist without our interference. If one dog is clearly more dominant than the others, we should anticipate and satisfy its need to be first. We can feed it first and let it go outside first, for example, to perpetuate its confidence and perception of leadership over the other dogs.

We have to maintain sufficient leadership over all dogs in the family so we can come between them if competition arises. We should not permit a dominant dog to steal food from the others. If necessary we should stand between the dogs to protect the rights of the more submissive ones. We should anticipate situations that are likely to result in competition and be prepared either to prevent them or prevent the fights that may result.

Those of us who live with more than one dog should seek compromises in our lifestyles that reinforce positive reactions between these dogs and discourage excessive competition. Every situation varies slightly, so it may be necessary to create individual solutions. One compromise worked very well for two spayed female schnauzers.

The family got the second schnauzer as a companion for the first one. The older dog had always been fairly dominant. It was aggressive toward strangers, and it became extremely dominant toward the other dog as soon as it moved in. This competitive reaction caused the second dog to chew on objects in the home when the owners were absent. At first, the younger dog would only chew on objects that were on the floor. With time, it began to pull books and objects off shelves and tables to chew them.

The owners gave the younger dog tranquilizers when they were gone, but this was unsuccessful. They locked it inside a small cage, but it attacked the bars of the cage with its teeth and claws. They usually restricted both dogs to one area of the house while they were away, but they made the mistake of locking them into increasingly smaller areas. This isolation backfired when the younger dog began to chew up the woodwork.

The owners blamed the younger dog for all the problems. That actually helped the older dog to excessively dominate the younger one. They were able to stop the chewing problem when they realized that the younger dog was merely reacting to this domination. They reversed their attitude toward the two dogs and came up with a compromise solution that worked well during their absences.

Most important, the owners began to treat both dogs equally and stopped permitting the older dog to steal food or territory from the younger one. This helped improve the second dog's confidence level without reducing the first dog's confidence. Since the younger dog needed more territory rather than less, they divided the house in half and let each dog live separately during their absences. Since they knew that eventually both dogs should learn to get along together, they began to provide them with equal access to the whole house.

At first, they left both dogs alone together for fifteen minutes at a time. When they returned home, they praised both dogs for tolerating their absence. They increased the time by half-hour and hour intervals until the dogs were able to live together by themselves for extended periods without competition or behavior problems. Eventually, both dogs had access to the entire house at all times, and they co-existed comfortably.

Many behavior specialists recommend getting a companion pet for a dog with behavior problems. It is true that dogs benefit from interrelationships with their own kind, but this is not recommended in situations where people are actually causing the first dog's behavior problems. That home will likely cause problems for the second dog as well.

Interactions with Cats

A young spayed female Saint Bernard named Pepper was displaying submissive behavior problems. She was a submissive wetter and would lose control during any frightening situation. Pepper was hyperactive and unpredictable, and she licked her left front leg so much that she got a large, swollen sore called a lick granuloma on her leg. Pepper passed an obedience training class with flying colors but continued to cause problems for herself and her owners. Behavior modification drug therapy was not helpful.

There were several reasons for Pepper's behavior. She was only eight months old and she was naturally submissive. Her owner blamed her for everything that went wrong. She showed the dog no leadership and panicked whenever a problem arose. The most harmful thing she did was to let the two household cats dominate Pepper at all times. Pepper was losing so much confidence that she continued to wet submissively and to mutilate herself by licking her leg. The cats had such a powerful effect on her behavior that the drug therapy that was usually successful did little good.

The average cat has more self-confidence than the average dog. Like their wild relatives, many pet cats imagine themselves to be king of beasts. Some cats are submissive and fearful, and they spend a lot of their lives hiding under the bed. Some cats can develop excellent relationships with dogs. They can sometimes learn to play, sleep, and live together as well as any two dogs. But the majority of cats feel a strong need to dominate dogs and they can cause many problems.

Ginger, the neutered cocker spaniel-dachshund female described earlier, has a very different life when she returns home, an example of the problems that can arise between cats and dogs.

Ginger is a confident dog with a fairly even mixture of dominant and submissive instincts. As proof of her dominant tendencies, she likes to jump up on people and pull on her leash. If she escapes her outside chain, she roams great distances through her neighborhood. She lived alone on a farm for six years and developed a great deal of survival confidence through her experiences. She caught and killed several wild animals that wandered too close to the farmhouse.

Ginger's behavior changed completely when she came to live in an urban home run by two cats. She hid under a table next to the owner's favorite chair and refused to come out. She let the cats steal her food, and she began to act increasingly depressed. The dominant male cat, Tory, would look down from the top of the table to glare at Ginger, and the female cat, Tuffy, would walk back and forth past the table just to hiss at her. Some dogs take only so much dominance from cats before their frustrations make them bite, or even kill the cats, but Ginger just became more depressed.

Several things had to be done quickly to balance the relationship and prevent Ginger from demonstrating extremes of submissive behavior. The owner sat down with all three animals and told them he loved them all. He said he wanted them to get along, and that he would intervene when the cats dominated Ginger too much. He promised to help all three fulfill their survival needs, and he made some changes around the house:

1. The owner knew Ginger needed more inside territory, so he put a blanket on the floor some distance from her table and coaxed her to lay on it. He told her, "This is Ginger's blanket." After the cats made Ginger retreat to her table, they sprayed their anal sac material onto the blanket. The owner physically ran the cats off the blanket and said, "No, this is Ginger's blanket." He sat down again and Tory walked back toward the

blanket. Because she had the owner's support, Ginger ran toward Tory and growled at him, and he walked away. She used her blanket from then on, and she could walk throughout the house without fear.

2. The owner decided to feed Ginger in a closet. He kept the door closed so the cats could not steal the food. He continued to feed Tory first, then Tuffy and Ginger, so Tory would know he was number one. Over time, the cats became less conscious of Ginger and her food, and Ginger gained confidence so she could eat her food with the closet door open.

3. Ginger was frustrated in the home since she had little opportunity to utilize her dominant instincts. The owner began giving her rawhide bones which she devoured one after another. Dominating bones helped relieve her frustrations inside the home. She sometimes saved small pieces of the bones to toss around or munch on at another time. The owner also provided Ginger with a regular schedule of attention by playing games with her where she would fetch bones for him.

4. The owner knew Ginger was confident when she wasn't with the cats, so he took her on car rides, gave her a long leash to use in the back yard, took her on two or three daily walks and took her back to the farm occasionally so she could get some exercise and explore old haunts. These were things the owner did with Ginger that he did not do with the cats.

5. The owner equalized his treatment of all three animals. He rarely gave snacks, but when he did, he gave each animal one treat at the same time. He made sure to spend a certain amount of time each day alone with each animal. If one seemed envious, he would tell it he loved it and that its turn would come. Whenever he left or returned home, he acknowledged all three animals with equal emphasis. When he went to bed at night, he told each animal he loved it.

6. The owner knew some sort of leadership ladder had to be maintained to prevent competitive chain reactions. He knew Tory would have to be permitted to think he was king so he would have no need to dominate the other animals. He satisfied Tory's dominant needs by letting him dominate the owner. He let Tory get up on his lap to sleep, to lick his hands and chin,

and basically to let him think he was superior. The owner knew if he competed too much with Tory's need to claim superiority, Tory would begin to dominate and beat up on Tuffy. She in turn would develop a bladder infection and take out her frustrations on Ginger. Ginger would return to her depressed, submissive state.

Ginger, Tory and Tuffy are not the most compatible housemates, but their owner fulfilled his responsibilities on a daily basis, and all three pets now accept each other's presence without complaint. They sometimes even act friendly toward each other. Perhaps coincidentally, all three animals have remained as physically healthy as they have remained behaviorally balanced.

Competitive reactions still occur on occasion, but these incidents are usually mild and of little consequence. Tory likes to sleep on the owner's favorite spot on the couch. The owner sensed this preference and said to Tory, "Don't get on my spot, I'll be back" when he left the couch for a moment. Before he could return, Ginger began to bark at him. She acted like she wanted him to follow her. Ginger walked right up to Tory, touched him with her nose, and barked at him. He had curled up on the owner's favorite spot.

Another time, a loud noise awakened the owner. He thought one of the cats had knocked something over accidently so he tried to ignore it, but Ginger began to bark at him again. She led him to the chair where Tuffy was hiding and her actions said, "It was Tuffy that made the noise." Tuffy hissed and snapped her paw at Ginger as if to say, "How dare you tell on me."

Responsible, consistent, balanced, equal, and loving leadership can help dogs and cats coexist. It can turn major problems into minor ones, and it can prevent many problems altogether.

Chapter 14

DRUG THERAPY
AND TRAINING DEVICES

Some behaviorists and veterinarians recommend behavior-altering medications and/or a variety of training aids to control behavior problems in dogs. There are dogs and people that can benefit from these drugs and devices, but many more dogs do not benefit.

A few dogs are truly neurotic and psychotic. Schizophrenia and other more bizarre psychological maladies have also been identified on occasion. A few dogs are born with combinations of dominant and submissive instincts that make them unable to exist in human society. Other dogs either inherit or contract brain disorders which adversely affect their behavior. These dogs may need drug therapy to modify and balance their instincts so they can live among people.

All dogs should receive regular examinations from veterinarians, and those with behavior problems should be examined further to make sure that health problems aren't responsible for the behavior change. There are some excellent procedures that combine long-term drug therapy with behavior modification to help many dogs with neurological and psychological defects live a more normal life, but most dog behavior problems are not the result of physical or mental impairment.

We can give a tranquilizer to a dog that is afraid of thunderstorms to help it tolerate the storm better. This helps temporarily, but it doesn't help the dog overcome its fear. We can give a dominant dog a tranquilizer or another drug to keep it from biting us, but that doesn't correct whatever caused the biting. If we force a dog to live in a drug-induced state just to keep it from bothering us, that is unnecessary and expensive and does the dog no good whatsoever.

The real problem with drug therapy is that it helps us without helping our dogs. If we really love our dogs, we should try to resolve simple instinctive conflicts without resorting to drug therapy. Many of these problems are as much our fault as the dog's.

We must consider our long-term relationship with our dog. If we rely on drug therapy to control certain problems, the problems will continue, if not worsen, so we must plan on using drug therapy throughout the dog's life. If we try to correct the problem when it arises, chances are we can prevent it from happening again and can improve the long-term relationship. When we hesitate to take positive, direct action, we permit the problem to perpetuate itself. If it becomes habitual, we may have no choice but to use drug therapy, or worse, to get rid of the dog. Drug therapy has its place in behavior modification therapy, but dogs benefit most when their owners take the time to develop a positive interpersonal relationship with them.

There are many drugs, devices, and procedures which can be used to prevent pregnancy in dogs. Some of these drugs can also modify sexual behavior on a short-term basis and are used routinely by some therapists. Long-term drug therapy is expensive, but is useful in some circumstances. Vaginal prostheses and tubal ligations in females and vasectomies in males do a good job controlling pregnancy, but they do nothing to modify behavior. Neutering is a one-time procedure that works best of all at preventing pregnancy and controlling sexual behavior.

Many training devices are available commercially and are widely used. These include choke collars, shock collars, and ultrasound devices which have all been shown to induce behavior change. Some of these devices can cause unnecessary pain and injury to dogs, and they can never totally replace human love and understanding in preventing and controlling dog behavior problems.

Choke and shock collars help us use extra force to control dog behavior. This implies that those of us who use these devices cannot serve a leadership role by ourselves. The kind of a relationship we have with a dog is questionable if we must make it feel pain whenever it misbehaves. Since a dog can obey orders from a confident leader, it would be better for the dog and us if we try to increase our own confidence levels rather than to decrease the dog's confidence through constant punishment. If we use these devices, that implies that we do not trust our dogs to obey our commands without the threat of punishment. This is not the loving, sharing kind of relationship that is most beneficial.

Ultrasound devices can be effective in modifying specific dog behaviors. An ultrasound device makes a sound too high-pitched for us to hear, but dogs hear it and are irritated by it. If they hear the sound when they misbehave, they will learn to change the behavior to keep from hearing the sound. These devices may be especially helpful in dealing with habitual problems and with dogs that have one or two particularly disturbing behaviors.

If we select the right animals in the first place and then develop and maintain a balanced relationship, extra training devices are unnecessary. We are born with all the tools we need to interact favorably with dogs; we have to learn what we have and then practice until we are confident. When we do this, behavior problems usually solve themselves.

Chapter 15

SURVIVAL CONFLICTS—
THE TOUGH DECISIONS

There are times when we cannot or will not take the steps necessary to improve a dog's behavior. There are dogs whose genetic makeup or environmental trauma make them incompatible with human society. If we cannot let certain dogs continue to live with us, we may have to make some tough decisions.

There are several alternatives available although some of them are not viable. No dog should be kicked out of a home or abandoned. No matter how much suffering we think certain dogs have caused us, we cause them to suffer far more when we force them to survive on their own in a complex, potentially hostile society. Some may survive, but most suffer greatly and may die horrible deaths. Most pet dogs no longer have the ability to survive without human assistance.

It is reasonable to offer a dog to another family. We should interview prospective new owners to determine who might be most compatible with our dog. More than anything, we should tell prospective owners the exact nature of the problems we have had with the dog. They should know these problems ahead of time and be convinced that they can tolerate or hopefully improve the dog's behavior. We might find new owners more quickly by lying or hiding the unpleasant truths, but we would do the dog and the new owners a great disservice. It may take time to find the right family for a particular dog, but if we want to help a dog we should place it with the best possible alternative family.

Since many people select the wrong dog in the first place, there are many people who must look for housing alternatives for their dogs. There's a good chance that someone else has a dog that would fit in better in our family than theirs, and we may have the dog they would find more suitable.

Another alternative is to give a dog to a humane society or

animal shelter. It is very important to provide the shelter with a complete physical and behavioral history. Since there are more dogs than dog owners, many dogs in humane societies and animal shelters are eventually put to sleep permanently. Many more dogs are there because of behavior problems that may repeat themselves after a subsequent adoption. A complete history can help a shelter counsel prospective owners to select dogs that are compatible with their homes and personalities. Failure to do this is almost always harmful to the dog and the new owners.

Euthanasia is always a possibility. Putting a dog to sleep permanently instead of letting it die on its own raises moral questions that few, if any, of us can answer accurately. If we examine a dog's quality of life and degree of suffering, there are situations where euthanasia might be considered humane. If a dog has behavioral tendencies which make it incompatible with human society, it suffers when it is forced to live with us. If a dog has owners who create survival conflicts for it, euthanasia may be a more viable alternative than forcing it to continue to survive in that environment. If a dog has no control over its behavioral extremes, the destructiveness of these extremes can cause it to suffer a great deal. Some people feel euthanasia prevents a dog from suffering needlessly.

Some situations must make us consider alternatives to dog ownership. Some dogs are too dangerous to live around people. Some are born with too many dominant tendencies to accept leadership from people. Other dogs are reinforced to continue aggressive tendencies until biting and other behaviors become especially purposeful and self-fulfilling.

A two-year-old male mixed breed dog was so aggressive from birth that neutering did little to calm it down. It bit several people, including the family's three children, on numerous occasions. Euthanasia was finally arranged, but the decision was delayed for several weeks because one of the children had trouble accepting it. During the delay, the dog bit three more people. This dog was too dangerous to live with this or most any family.

Behavior problems that become habitual can be extremely

difficult to correct. Dogs that learn to housesoil or chew furniture may continue to do so despite behavior modification therapy. These dogs are permitted to become too asocial to live in most homes.

Habitual problems may not entirely be the owner's fault. A three-year-old male unneutered German shepherd was always nervous. This dog would literally go crazy during thunderstorms. When the owners were not home, if there was a sudden storm, the dog would destroy the whole household. Even when they were there, the owners found it difficult to restrain and reassure the hundred-pound dog.

When the dog was younger, lightning struck within 500 yards of the dog's home. This terribly traumatic experience increased the dog's fears to unmanageable levels. Neutering, playing records of thunderstorms, and drug therapy were all unsuccessful. The dog was finally put to sleep permanently.

Dogs with specific neurological and severe physical problems may benefit most from euthanasia if veterinary therapy fails to reduce their suffering. Some dogs are born with unusual or incompatible mixtures of dominant and submissive tendencies. A few dogs are so unstable that they may be dominant when they should be submissive and vice versa. Some can only utilize extremes of behavior, with no middle ground possible.

A five-year-old collie-German shepherd cross had extremely unpredictable behavior. It was very high-strung and nervous, although the owner was able to help the dog calm down on most occasions. Once in a while, for no predictable reason, the dog would attack its owner. This happened most often when the owner tried to reach down to take something away from the dog. These unpredictably extreme episodes each lasted less than a minute and mimicked mild epileptic seizures. A neurologist found no evidence of epilepsy but noticed a conflict situation. The dog would be submissive and loving part of the time, then it would revert to an extremely dominant, aggressive mode at other times (especially to protect possessions). The dog had no ability to modify its extremes, so euthanasia was necessary.

Since the process by which we select pet dogs tends to favor submissive followers over dominant, independent dogs, many submissive dogs are bred to each other. The offspring of these inbreeding situations can be too submissive for their own good. They may be too fearful, self-destructive, and dependent and require too much attention and physical contact. No one person can fulfill all the needs of dogs like these at all times, and dogs must be able to help themselves on occasion to maintain survival confidence and a will to live. These dogs destroy themselves with time, and they suffer a great deal while they are alive.

Old dogs may suffer from senility and, hence, irreversible damage to the brain and surrounding membranes. Senility may cause a dog to seek more frequent companionship, to become excessively fearful, to run into things and demonstrate periodic confusion, and to forget previous housetraining. The untrained eye may misinterpret these changes as correctable behavior problems, but punishment or attempts at behavior modification only make the dog more fearful and confused. In such cases, our failure to accept these changes without overreaction can lead to a dog's rapid demise. Acceptance or euthanasia may be our only alternatives for senile dogs.

Most often, dogs are given up for adoption or are put to sleep permanently because their survival needs conflict with the needs of their owners. Some people refuse to function as leaders for their dogs, and others are convinced they cannot change their own nature enough to fulfill their responsibilities. Some dog owners are allergic to dogs. Some people have trouble deciding what role dogs should play in their lives. Some families argue constantly over how individual family members should behave toward their dogs.

The number of potential survival conflicts is infinite. Each case is different and requires a different solution. The following case histories describe some of these conflicts and the alternatives that were selected:

Case 1: A one-year-old cocker spaniel male lived alone with a woman whose job required her to be absent for weeks at a time. She boarded the dog in a kennel during these absences, but the dog began to bite her when she was home. She felt the dog was getting back at her for leaving it in a kennel so much. Whether this was true or not, the owner realized she did not have the time to become a consistent leader for the dog and she gave it up for adoption.

Case 2: A nine-month-old female great dane had an instinctive conflict between her natural curiosity and episodes of intense fear. She would nose into things, then jump and run away nervously when the object of her curiosity moved. The owner planned to use her as a show dog, but the dog was extremely fearful of show judges and all the people involved in breed shows. The dog was most fearful during its first heat period.

The owner realized that the dog made a good pet. She felt she could help it get over fears in the home. She also realized that neutering might reduce some of the dog's fears and help balance its behavior. A champion show dog must be intact and be able to reproduce, so the owner was in conflict over how best to utilize her pet.

The woman had two alternatives, and she ended up using both. First, she hired an experienced show dog handler to train her dog out of its fears. When that didn't work, she had it neutered. Even if neutering had not helped the dog's behavior, the owner knew it would prevent offspring that might have similar instinctive conflicts. The woman gave up her dream of breeding champion show dogs, but she ended up with an excellent pet.

Case 3: A woman who was allergic to dogs owned an older mixed breed male dog, a cross between a poodle and a terrier. The woman's allergy problem was getting worse as she got older, and she was particularly intolerant of her dog sleeping with her. To protect her own health, the woman started locking the dog out of her bedroom. In response, the dog began to urinate and defecate on the floor near the bedroom and to scratch the bedroom door. This was a predictable reaction to sudden isolation, but the woman felt she had no choice but to keep the dog out of her bedroom.

Since the dog was beginning to show senile changes anyway, the woman decided on euthanasia. Better than that, she made a firm commitment not to own more dogs, a decision that ended her conflict permanently.

Case 4: A ten-year-old female Scottie was wetting in the home. The wife was convinced the dog lost control at these times, but her husband, a psychologist who analyzed people, was convinced that the dog was doing it on purpose and punished it physically for every mistake, whether or not he caught the dog in the act.

The owners were unwilling to compromise their beliefs even though their competition and inconsistency probably made the dog's problem worse. Attitude adjustment, understanding, and love may have done wonders for the dog's behavior, but the owners had it put to sleep permanently.

Case 5: An eight-year-old intact male cairn terrier normally slept with his owner. For some reason, the woman kicked him off the bed one night. After she left for work the next day, the dog shredded her bed sheets. When she saw this destruction, the woman hit him and locked him out of the bedroom. When the dog repeated his destructive behavior in another bedroom the next day, the woman decided to close all doors. When she mistakenly left the den door open, the dog went in and completely destroyed a large couch. The dog was then locked in the bathroom, where the woman tape-recorded the dog barking and howling during her absences.

It should be obvious that this is a typical chain reaction which results from competition between a dog and its owner. Even though an attitude adjustment was called for, the woman had many personal insecurities and doubted her ability for constructive change. She was so frustrated that she was considering euthanasia.

Fortunately, as a last resort, the woman decided to find her dog another home by putting advertisements in several newspapers. Although she doubted anyone would want an older dog with behavior problems, a man called her and asked if he could have it. His fifteen-year-old cairn terrier had just passed away, and he understood and loved that breed. He was retired and lived alone, so he was convinced the dog would find his home to be a favorable environment. The dog lived with the man from then on, and it had no further problems.

There are times when we must face some harsh realities.

Some people cannot be good leaders for dogs, and some are too selfish to accept the responsibilities of leadership. These people should understand themselves well enough not to get dogs in the first place. There are a few dogs that do not make good pets and we are unfair to force them to live with or around people. Sometimes we have to make difficult decisions.

But before we decide to give up our dogs or have them put to sleep, we should reevaluate our roles in their behavior problems. All dog owners have problems with their dogs from time to time, but most of us can keep these problems to a minimum. Most dogs with behavior problems are not sick but are reacting normally and predictably to changes in their environment frequently caused by their owners.

We want dogs to adapt their behavior to our lifestyles, but we cannot expect dogs to adapt better to us than we do to them. If anything, as leaders we should be even more adaptable than dogs. Adaptation requires some sacrifices and specific personal changes on our parts. The more inflexible we are, the fewer the number of dogs that are compatible with us. Short-term sacrifices can pay innumerable dividends in the long run.

Chapter 16

IMPROVED HEALTH THROUGH BEHAVIORAL CONTENTMENT

There is a definite relationship between behavior and health. The degree of association is debatable, but it exists nonetheless. There is no question that dogs that are forced to go against their natural instincts, and those born with extremes of tendencies, are susceptible to numerous diseases and physical injuries. If we help dogs remain balanced behaviorally, we can help prevent many health problems.

Some health considerations have been discussed previously. To reiterate: excessively dominant or excessively submissive dogs are self-destructive. A highly dominant dog may walk in front of a car because it imagines itself superior to all other forces in nature. It gets into many fights to prove its dominance, so it risks frequent injury. The need to roam, explore, and dominate objects in their territory can cause dominant dogs to enter areas where they can be injured or come in contact with poisons. They want to handle their own problems, so they may resist human assistance, including veterinary care. They may not protect themselves during sickness; if they continue to engage in their daily activities despite illness, they can become even more ill.

The submissive extreme causes dogs to injure themselves in a variety of ways. If excessive fear induces panic, dogs will react opposite to their needs and increase the likelihood of injury or illness. Submissive dogs may bite and scratch themselves excessively, either from frustration, boredom, a need for physical stimulation, or reaction to a disease or injury. Self-mutilation is destructive and can lead to skin diseases and lick granulomas. If not treated quickly, these skin diseases can sometimes spread to the rest of the body and can cause severe illness.

A male unneutered great dane was submissive by nature and lived with people who misunderstood it. Through a combination of environmental stress (owner competition) and mating seasons, the dog began to mutilate itself. It licked one of its rear legs until a lick granuloma resulted. A veterinarian surgically removed the lick granuloma on two occasions, but it returned each time because the causes of the problem still existed. The dog started licking a front leg and its scrotum until both became red, swollen, and inflamed. It licked its own rectum until raw, and it rubbed its anal sacs against the floor until they abscessed and drained pus. The dog also masturbated by licking its penis and it developed an inflamed prostate gland, but it never did these things when its owners were present.

Through a combination of neutering and owner attitude adjustment, the dog stopped mutilating itself. All the injuries healed and never returned. Behavioral and environmental adjustments improved the dog's health immeasurably.

Stress is a major contributing factor to a number of diseases in animals as well as people. Any kind of stress can weaken a body's natural defense mechanisms, making it more susceptible to invading bacteria, viruses, and other microorganisms. In people, sudden temperature changes are enough of a stress to cause colds and many other diseases, and the same is true of dogs. Recent research indicates that stress is a major factor in the onset of cancer and its ability to spread to other body parts in mice and probably in dogs and people. A stressful relationship between dog and human may actually increase the possibility of cancer in both parties.

Dogs undergo behavioral stress when they are forced to live in environments incompatible with their nature. They feel stress if they are not permitted to be themselves. A pet dog with a need to follow people meets with stress when it is forced or permitted to take over leadership in the home. The nervousness associated with the threat of having to care for itself can cause a natural follower dog great stress. By the same token, a dominant dog is equally upset when it is forced to submit to a domineering person at all times or is confined to a small cage or territory. These dogs feel stress because they cannot fulfill their own instinctive needs.

Young puppies are exposed to stress when they are forced to

move from one home to another, from a puppy mill to a pet store. Mating seasons are always stressful times for intact dogs. Dogs are faced with numerous stress situations, and these can be as damaging to a dog's physical health as they are to its behavior.

When a dog has self-confidence, it is usually behaviorally sound and has a strong will to live. Perhaps there is a direct association between confidence level and health. A confident dog is usually healthy, and it often has physical problems when it loses confidence. If it loses too much confidence, it loses the will to live. Once an animal has lost the will to live, there isn't a veterinarian in the world who can keep it alive.

A two-year-old female Yorkshire terrier became depressed, lethargic, and dehydrated for no apparent reason. A complete physical examination showed the dog to be completely healthy, although the dog certainly looked and acted sick. The dog was treated symptomatically and was given fluids to correct the dehydration.

When the dog stopped eating, the owners prepared a moist gruel from its usual gourmet diet and force-fed the dog with it. They hoped to keep up the dog's strength, but the procedure backfired when some of the dog food splattered and dried on the dog's face. This caused a skin irritation which made the dog scratch its face until it was raw, and both eyes became infected.

The dog's general condition was getting worse. Repeated examinations could not determine a diagnosis. Repeated fluid therapy was unsuccessful since the dog would become dehydrated again within just a couple hours after massive fluid therapy. Despite frequent veterinary attention, the dog was getting weaker.

The owners were about ready to give up because of the dog's apparent suffering and the great expense of caring for it. As a last resort, they decided to test the dog's will to live. It had been spoiled and pampered since it was a puppy, and it had grown to expect its owners to fulfill all its needs. Perhaps the force-feeding was wrong because it reinforced this notion and caused the dog not to eat or care for itself.

Since the family also owned a small mixed breed dog that was not pampered and ate dry food, the decision was made to force the Yorkie to compete with the other dog for its dry food. All feedings were stopped, and the dog was forced to fend for itself in the home.

If the dog had no will to live, it was senseless to continue any therapy. Forcing it to either die or compete with the other dog for food, without any pampering, was a good test of its will to live. Not surprisingly, the Yorkie accepted this change readily. It got its own food and its health improved completely within one day. A better relationship with the family helped prevent further health problems. The dog's will to live improved because it was helping itself for a change.

Speculative Considerations

Because there are so many situations where health and behavior are related, one might wonder how strong this relationship really is. Whenever a dog has behavior problems or loses confidence, health problems can become a secondary complication. Might the opposite also be true? Can we improve a dog's health by balancing its behavioral extremes, helping it fulfill its instinctive needs, and improving its self-confidence?

We have seen how dominant and submissive instincts are opposites, that they are both present in all dogs and that they function best when they are used on an alternating basis. Perhaps this alternating instinctive interrelationship also explains the migration patterns of numerous animal, bird, and insect species that alternately escape from and return to their place of birth. These opposite instincts might also control the internal functioning of an animal's body. A fearful, submissive dog that is backed into a corner and cannot escape externally still has an intense need to get free. Many of these dogs lose bladder and bowel control under these circumstances. Perhaps they "escape" internally because they cannot escape externally.

When we look closely at a dog's body, we find that it functions because of checks and balances based on opposites. Dogs eat, but they also defecate. Dogs drink, but they also urinate. They inhale air to breathe, but they also exhale. The brain sends nerve impulses throughout the body, but it also receives equal input from all body parts. The heart sends blood throughout the body, but it receives blood in return. Muscles in a dog's appendages perform the opposite tasks of flexing and extending joints on an alternating basis. The body cannot function properly without this balance of opposites.

These opposite body functions sound similar to dominant and submissive instincts. One must wonder if perhaps both behavior and physiology somehow function on the basis of the same opposing forces. If all functioning is the result of two opposite instinctive drives, then it makes sense that if we help the mind we are also helping the body, and vice versa.

When a dog is sick, its spirit and confidence level sag. When we improve the dog's health, it feels better so its confidence improves. It might also be true that if we improve a dog's spirit, its health will improve as well. If so, we can improve a dog's health and prolong its lifespan simply by helping it develop behavioral contentment by letting it be itself and by balancing its instinctive needs.

Chapter 17

FROM LEADERSHIP TO EQUALITY

Dogs respond instinctively to changes in their environment. They use either dominant or submissive behaviors to fulfill their instinctive needs, and both sets of behaviors are present. Dogs with extremes of behavior are self-destructive and may be unsuitable as pets. But the vast majority of dogs can be excellent pets if their needs are balanced by people who understand and love them.

Since most dogs are bred for their willingness to follow human leaders, we have a tremendous responsibility to serve as confident leaders for dogs. We need to understand our role with dogs and to understand how we can contribute to their behavioral changes, and we need to accept our own errors so that improvements can be made when necessary.

We also need to understand a dog's true nature. We must realize that dogs function best when they are accepted for their right to exist and are permitted to be themselves. We need to see the world from a dog's perspective, how it normally behaves, and how it perceives us. We need to let dogs be dogs and to understand their own levels. Perhaps understanding is reached when we realize how often we can hurt dogs as well as how often they can hurt us. Since understanding ourselves and our dogs can only help, there should be no reason why we should fear or resist opportunities for better understanding.

Understanding leadership is important because dogs look to us for leadership. Leadership does not imply constant dominance or permissiveness toward dogs.

It requires a willingness to dominate at times and to submit at times so a dog isn't forced into an extreme perspective but has its confidence level and instinctive needs balanced. We should neither parent a dog nor behave like a child toward it. We should utilize a confident adult ego state and treat dogs as adults also.

What our leadership really requires is that we treat dogs as equals. If we force a dog to submit at all times, it will perceive itself as inferior and lose confidence. If we let a dog dominate us, we are admitting our own inferiority and are preventing a dog from fulfilling its dependent needs. In either case, we do a dog a disservice and cause it to suffer both behavior and health problems.

When we act dominant toward a dog that needs us to do so, we are giving dominance out of love, like a parent to a child. When we submit to a dog in order to reinforce its confidence, we are giving submissive love. It makes sense then that if we give both dominant love and submissive love to a dog at the proper times, we are offering it more love than it could possibly receive otherwise. If we treat a dog as an equal, we admit that we love it as much as we love ourselves. For most of us, this is a great deal of love.

If we give this much love, a dog is bound to have self-confidence because all its needs are being fulfilled, especially its need for love. People function better when their self-confidence is boosted, so giving our love to a dog may offer a similar reward.

When we give love based on equality, we might be able to increase a dog's potential as its confidence level rises. Some dogs act dumb and relatively worthless, especially when their owners assume they are dumb and worthless. Some dogs act extremely intelligent and perform some amazing tasks. Perhaps we can increase apparent intelligence in dogs simply by treating them with respect and assuming they are capable rather than incapable.

Since we can only modify and not totally change a dog's nature, our acceptance of this reality also offers dogs the love of equality because they have no choice but to accept us in the same way. We should love a dog enough not to force perfection or human values on it. Dogs simply do not do well when they are forced to act like people rather than like dogs.

The main reason we live with dogs is the strong bond of attraction that exists between many people and many dogs. This bond is natural rather than acquired; a dog's love cannot be earned if there is no natural loving bond between the dog and its owner. That is why proper selection of a pet is so important. If a dog does not sense a natural attraction with its new owner from the beginning, problems are certain to result.

Dogs need love, but so do we. We can benefit from our relationship with dogs just as much as they can, but we can receive no more love from dogs than we are willing to give. If we give the most love by treating a dog as an equal, we can receive the most love and warmth in return.

We need love, but we also enjoy it. Love can be fun, so there is no reason to ignore or compete against the natural attractions that exist between people and dogs. With love, both dogs and people benefit, as their other needs become less important. Until we turn to other people for love, dogs can always help us fulfill our love needs. If we give of ourselves to our dogs, we will receive at least as much love in return.

This book has tried to explore the relationship between dogs and people and the ways we can help dogs remain behaviorally sound. It explored generalities that seem to apply to all human-dog relationships, but it could not describe every possible situation that exists. Ultimately, we must adapt our understanding of dogs to the situations at hand and arrive at conclusions on our own. No one can give us a guaranteed list of procedures that will work with all dogs at all times.

Perhaps our role with dogs is summarized best by a prayer, paraphrased here:

"Grant us the courage to accept those things we cannot change, the strength to change the things we can, and the wisdom to know the difference."

BIBLIOGRAPHY

Campbell, William E. *Behavior Problems in Dogs*. Santa Barbara: American Veterinary Publications, Inc., 1975.

Fox, Michael W. *Understanding Your Dog*. New York: Bantam Books, 1974.

Sautter, Frederic J., & John A. Glover. *Behavior, Development, and Training of the Dog*. New York: Arco Publishing Company, Inc., 1978.

Scott, John Paul, & John L. Fuller. *Dog Behavior, the Genetic Basis*. Chicago: The University of Chicago Press, 1965.